MANAGEMENT AND MORALITY

Also by John Adair:

Hastings to Culloden (co-author)

Training for Leadership

Roundhead General
   A Biography of Sir William Waller

Training for Decisions

Action-Centred Leadership

Training for Communication

Cheriton, 1644
   The Campaign and the Battle

MANAGEMENT AND MORALITY

MORALITY

*The Problems and Opportunities
of Social Capitalism*

John Adair

DAVID & CHARLES
NEWTON ABBOT LONDON VANCOUVER

0 7153 6500 2

Set in 11 on 13pt Plantin
and printed in Great Britain
by W. J. Holman Limited, Dawlish
for David & Charles (Holdings) Limited
South Devon House, Newton Abbot, Devon

Contents

Foreword

The purpose of this book is to stimulate thought about the nature of our society and the profession of management within it. The first five chapters are general in scope, drawing out and sifting the main values which influence the direction and character of contemporary business life. These values hold together in an emerging philosophy which I have called social capitalism.

In contrast, the last five chapters are much more practical and personal in approach. They review some of the more likely or possible developments in the immediate future for making business morally better which are already under discussion, such as codes of ethics, changes in company law and management education. Because the broad tides influencing the ethos of business are as much social and personal as professional, we should not pin too many hopes on these particular reforms.

What is certain is that the gradual social movement towards a more moral stance will continue. And our present uncertainties, springing from the unfinished nature of social capitalism, will place a high premium on personal integrity in management leadership. Upon these sure foundations, managers throughout the world can now reach out towards a much richer understanding of their calling. My concluding chapters map some of the possible paths forward for management as a whole, but I have judged it right to finish the book with an emphasis upon the challenges and costs of personal integrity.

My thanks are due to all the managers and businessmen in Britain, America, Europe and Africa with whom I have had the

Foreword

opportunity in these last five years to discuss the themes of leadership, decision-making, problem-solving and creative thinking, as well as the nature of our slowly evolving world society. I must also thank Simon Webley for permission to reproduce his diagrams in Chapter 7 and Hunter Davies of the *Sunday Times* for the article in Chapter 5.

J.A.

CHAPTER 1

The Profit Motive

The most common assumption about managers is still that they are in business solely to make a profit. Moreover, in traditional economics, the profit motive is held to be the basis of the capitalist or free enterprise system. Much verbal ammunition has been exchanged between those who defend the profit motive as moral, or at least amoral, and those who denounce it as downright immoral. For complex reasons they may both be right.

Profit comes from the Latin *profectus*, itself the noun from *proficere*, to advance. Thus profit is essentially a general word which has acquired some specific meanings. In this book I shall be using it primarily to mean the financial gain in any transaction. But what is gain? The origins of the verb 'to gain' in Old High German suggest that it may have once meant to pasture, to till the earth, to forage or to hunt for food. Thus the first 'gains' may have been the produce of nature which man won or gained by his labour in the fields or his skill as a hunter. Indeed 'gainage', an obsolete Middle English word, once stood for profit or produce from the tillage of land.

Religion enters on the scene in the earliest times, because it was widely believed that the great gap between man's puny efforts and the immeasurably abundant produce of field and forest could only be explained by the activity of gods or God, the mysterious sources of the annual plenty. Thus man may sow and reap, but it is God who gives the increase.

Profit or gains in this sense could be understood as God-given, natural and good. For the irruption of immorality into the picture we turn to the juxtaposition of a number of factors, such as the fact of morality, the fact of man's nature and the fact of money. For obviously profit in the sense of financial gains could not arise until money had been invented, somewhere around the year 700 BC.

RECIPROCITY AND THE PRIMITIVE ETHIC

Reciprocity means the alternating backwards and forwards movement of giving and receiving. It stands for the essential capacity and preference for interchange in mankind. When we say that man has a social nature it means that he is constituted to be both giver and receiver, that his survival and joy rest upon mutual exchange. Within the religious framework this reciprocity involved God as well as fellow men. Giving and receiving formed the core of personal life.

The primitive ethic, as it could be called, stands for the common sense that the backwards and forwards energies in human intercourse should be balanced in equilibrium, so that the exchange of gifts or dealings between two or more people is equal. Morality begins in the mutual feeling that this equivalence of exchange *ought* to exist, whether it does or not in particular cases.

This simple morality of a fair or just balance between forwards and backwards movement comes into play in the root forms of all business transactions known as barter. Barter is the exchange of commodities. It rests upon the characteristic of human reciprocity: the willingness to give and receive. The produce or products which are man's gain or profit from nature are traded for each other. The advantage of the system is that a degree of specialisation becomes possible: the hunter can exchange meat for the iron weapons of the smith. If both parties are satisfied by the equivalence of the two commodities, expressed by their willingness to do business again with each other, the bartering may be described as fair.

In this scheme of things a man did not make a profit out of his neighbour. He had already received this surplus or gain in the excess of nature's yield to him of the commodity or crops he specialised in producing. If nature had been exceptionally bountiful and he could exchange the surplus produce for more goods than his physical necessities required, he became wealthy.

In a religious society the danger of wealth lay in its power to reduce a man's sense of dependence on God. He could forget that his wealth had come directly from the gain that God had built into nature. The correct acknowledgement of that fact included the offering of sacrifice: portions of the surplus wealth of wine, corn and meat poured, offered or burnt back to God as a token that all the profit was his alone. The wealthy man could easily forget this duty, and turn from trusting in God to reposing his faith in full barns and great flocks of sheep, goats and camels. Moreover, such wealth multiplied naturally, adding to his preoccupation with worldly goods. Thus the Psalmist could caution his hearers: 'If riches increase, set not your heart upon them'.

We can perhaps trace in these pre-monetary days the genesis of the profit motive. The reciprocal primitive ethic led religious people to assume that the wealthy man had merited God's favour in some way. His earthly blessings were rewards for moral uprightness and active diligence. Thus the fundamental moral law of equivalence had not been broken, and the religious system of ideas remained intact despite some disturbing evidence that the wicked seemed to prosper (at least temporarily) under their 'green bay tree' while good men prayed for blessings in vain. What the religion of ancient Israel opposed was the tendency to seek wealth as an end itself, divorced from any sense of God as the author of all profit. This system, however, split like an old wineskin when money was poured into it.

THE EFFECTS OF MONEY

The introduction of money as a universal means of exchange was a gradual process, prefaced in different parts of the world by the use of such mediums as rare stones, shells, minerals and lumps or metals. Precious stones and metals gained favour in the early

11

centuries of history because they each possessed a unique cluster of characteristics which made them valuable, such as utility for tools or weapons, glitter, appeal to women and rarity. Even today we still use gold for filling teeth and diamonds for the points of industrial drills.

The early use of money rested on the same assumption of equi-value as barter: an early trader might bite the coin to test its metal, but he would assume that the goods were worth the intrinsic precious metal he had been handed. Despite its own internal evolution away from a metal basis, money has retained its essential character as a means of exchange for goods and services. Moreover, the link with metal has lasted into our own times, with the dollar worth so much gold and other currencies pegged in relation to it. Whether or not we shall ever move completely and successfully away from the gold standard remains to be seen.

The great relative value of jewels and coins being concentrated in such small spaces, like nuts, excited the acquisitive and hoarding instincts already latent in humanity, while at the same time a money economy with such unsuspected forces as the 'law of supply and demand' at play began to multiply the changes for financial gain. Here we return to the more familiar definition of profit as the monetary gain in a transaction. Where barter is a secondary activity of farmers and hunters, a means of exchanging one man's God-given surplus for another's on an equivalent basis, trading activity is more a method for disposing gains than a means of obtaining them. Money facilitated the rise of trade as a primary activity. The trader obtained a product at a cost and had to sell it at a certain price. We could call the difference between the two figures the merchant's profit or loss. In this book, however, I am following the practice of counting his wage into the costs. Quite how this wage should be assessed, of course, is open to endless debate, but let us assume for the time being that it can be determined. It is the difference between cost (including his wage) and the total financial return which constitutes the real profit or surplus value.

The Profit Motive

Now the moral objection in a personal society to real profit is simple. If one person is a gainer in a commercial transaction it follows that he makes the other into a loser. For he gets more than he gives. Thus the primitive ethic is disturbed. In a monetary system, of course, it is possible for this other person to recover his loss by passing it on to another unsuspecting neighbour. The assumption here is that wealth is essentially limited. It is true that wealth grows as more of nature's bounty, including gold, is gathered. But the population also has grown, so that there are more people to share in the increased wealth.

RELIGION AND MONEY

From an early stage all religions in the Near East developed a considerable vested interest in the continued existence of trading for pecuniary gain as opposed to equivalent bartering. The priesthood could persuade the rich to give money from their profits, which could be used for building and ornamenting temples and supporting elaborate choral worship. In ancient Israel, where Church and State were one, the religion shared fully in the common wealth of money gathered from the surplus value of individuals by taxes. The sale of sacrificial animals, and the exchange of money (at a profit) for this purchase, has become notorious because Jesus condemned these practices in the courtyard of the Jerusalem Temple, but relatively they were only minor sidelines. Organised religion and trading-for-profit flourished together.

As observers of the contemporary national scene, prophets such as Amos and Hosea noted that money still more than other means of exchange exerted an almost magical or religious power to draw men to its service and to induce them to put their trust in it for security. As such it was a concrete alternative to the invisible God, the God of Israel. They watched money exerting its quasi-magnetic influence on men, seducing them away from their true allegiance. In an age still infected with the animistic belief that everything—tree, brook and hill—had its own spirit, such a suspicion might have seemed natural enough. The frenzied worship of the Golden Calf, an object made from melted-down jewellery, illustrated the latent capacity in Israel for adoring gold as a god-like being, in total disregard for the God of Abraham, Isaac and Moses. This religious connection lives in our word *money*, which comes from *Moneta*, another name for the goddess Juno. The Romans first coined money in the Temple of Juno Moneta in Rome.

The prophets wove into their religious hatred of silver and gold idols numerous observations of the social consequences when some men gained wealth at the expense of their neighbours. A dark sense of the suffering caused as the greedy extorted from the poor and the strong ruthlessly fleeced the weak shadowed their message. For the prophets observed the tendency for the rich to grow richer, and the poor to get poorer. With the more socially acceptable malpractices of the powerful establishment marched such blatant contempts of the primitive ethic as bribery, cheating, fraud, robbery and murder.

The words of Jesus several hundred years after Amos, Hosea and Jeremiah appeared at first to be a repetition of their message. Certainly Jesus spoke out against wealth. He used the Aramaic word for riches *Mammon* as a symbol for all earth-bound influences that stood opposed to the Father of Israel. From this 'Mammon of unrighteousness' stemmed broken human relationships. But the message of Jesus was at once more positive and more revolutionary. Indeed, like the effects of a star explosion aeons ago, its waves of influence still reach us. And perhaps we have yet to comprehend fully what it means. Putting his message crudely and bluntly: whereas human nature had weighed down the *receiving* scale of that equilibrium dictated by the primitive ethic, Jesus thrust his hand into the other scale. In other words, he threw his weight into the side of *giving* at the expense of receiving.

For example, do not ask people to your party, if they can return the invitation—ask those who cannot invite you back. If a beggar asks for your coat, give him your cloak as well. The message of

Jesus could be here simply summarised: 'It is better to give than to receive.'

Yet Jesus seems to have retained the enlarged vision of the primitive ethic: God would balance the human loss from a value store not of this world. The man who gives freely will find his treasure in heaven, which is more secure than any earthly riches could ever be. Plentiful sowing brings a future spiritual harvest. These happy returns are bestowed by God, in this life or afterwards. As God has given more to man, and continues to pour out his gifts of value, so man should also give in like measure, with a God-like generosity to his neighbour—including the 'evil and ungrateful'—without hope of an equal return from him.

Therefore Jesus refused to act as judge in land or inheritance disputes; he spoke against 'all covetousness', and the fool who 'lays up treasure for himself and is not rich toward God'. Zacchaeus, a chief tax-collector in Jericho, showed that he had grasped the message by his response: 'The half of my goods I give to the poor, and if I have defrauded any one of any thing I restore it fourfold.'

Thus a powerful counter-thrust to the profit motive had entered human history. For it the Christians employed a special Greek word: *agape* or love, which was later translated into Latin as *caritas* and thence into English as *charity*. It summed up their reborn or aboriginal attitude, and led them into an early communist experiment of holding and distributing goods and services according to need. Any surplus money earned honestly went into the common purse, to be shared with the needy, especially those in 'the household of faith'.

But a great incentive to the new motive—the expected re-creation of the world and the coming of Christ in glory—just did not happen. The present order, with a money economy deeply entrenched, looked as if it would continue for an indeterminate period. Some limits of the 'give-more-than-you-receive' motive now had to be recognised.

The Profit Motive

Medieval Christendom rested upon compromise between world and gospel. The compromise line ran between the two mountains of profit and charity. The resulting balance could be called justice. But it was only the primitive ethic dressed up in Latin clothes. Buttressed by the Aristotelian doctrine of 'the golden mean', the Church of the late Roman Empire and Middle Ages set out to exact its part of the bargain from the worldly members who now crowded its naves, pulled in by decree, conquest and infant baptism as well as by the 'light of the Gospel'. Such folk could not be expected to practice Christian perfection like the holy hermits and saints, but they should observe the compromise principle of justice in their dealings with each other. In economic affairs this general ethic could be applied to interest, wages and prices.

The Law in the Bible had forbidden Jews to charge interest on loans to their own people, and the Church, encouraged by Aristotelian teaching on the barrenness of money, followed suit by condemning the practice as unlawful at the Third Lateran Council (1179). Like the just price and just wage it arose from the basic idea that justice requires that the seller should receive a value equivalent to that of the goods or services which he provides to the buyer. In practice, the medieval theologians recognised that the general conditions of supply and demand would be reflected in prices and wages, but they would not accept that the buyer's exceptional necessity gave the seller the right to exact a higher return. Extortionate prices in times of dearth received frequent condemnation. The just wage was the price of labour equal in value to the service provided by the seller to the buyer. In each type of occupation the pay had to be sufficient for the worker to maintain the status in society associated with his position in life.

The concept of status included duties as well as privileges. The Church could regulate the balance of wealth by encouraging the rich to observe the obligation of Christian charity. The primitive ethic in any society creates a certain pressure on the wealthy—those who have garnered a relatively large share of nature's excess

16

increase—to share their goods through gifts and feasts. Christianity baptised this natural equalising. The system had the merits of control and flexibility. The Church, compassionate, kept a hold on those sheep within its fold who could not even observe the natural law of justice, making them disgorge some of their ill-gotten gains to the poor as the price of a forward seat in purgatory. At the same time, the system recognised the element of unpredictability or unfairness in nature, which made some rich as much by lucky accident as by design. Such fortunates could reap their God-given harvest, and enjoy a rich but not luxurious life, providing they remembered the example of Zacchaeus in their closing years.

The prescriptions of medieval Christendom could be more easily observed in a slow-changing and predominantly agricultural society. But the changing conditions of the late Middle Ages rendered the compromise line ever more difficult to hold. The law against usury, like the law against adultery in later times, began to suffer the death of a thousand qualifications behind its solid scholastic façade of civil and canon law. The complex interactions of such factors as population, plague, the supply of precious metals and the beginnings of modern financing methods induced men to evade the laws on usury, prices and wages while continuing to pay lip service to them.

THE REFORMATION AND CAPITALISM

Luther's gigantic reaction to the medieval Church encompassed the money-grasping spirit within it which arose partly from the need to maintain a vast organisation. He began by condemning the sale of Indulgences. The purchase of these documents, it was claimed, would buy spiritual benefits in purgatory. The practice exhibited a twisted understanding of the Gospel concept that giving money away without hope of earthly return will be balanced by spiritual blessings. Luther objected to the notion that the popes had authority to settle such transactions. He also disliked its implicit claim for the power or status of money. Justification, however, came from God's inexplicable mercy to sinners: it could not be bought or sold, but accepted by faith alone.

For the man 'justified by faith alone' work became an expression of the new life of Christ within him. God's love reached out through the Christ in the believer to his near neighbours. Like Christ, the Christian must love his neighbour even to the point of sacrificing his salvation for him. God calls him to such costing love through a perception of the needs of others, which cry out to his skills for help. Unlike those useless drones in the monasteries, Luther taught, Christians exercised their vocations in all honest trades and occupations within the bustle and fever of the world. Risk and loss could therefore be welcomed with a courage born of faith. For the anxieties of human involvement would keep them mindful of their daily dependence upon the grace of God.

The Reformation coincided with some far-reaching changes in the economic spheres of finance, business organisation and trade. It is incorrect to say that the Reformation caused the rise of capitalism; more so, to claim that capitalism created the Reformation. But the two developments were related. Capitalism rested essentially on the use of accumulated wealth to finance production. A private capitalist is a person who has a surplus of money and invests it in business enterprise. He may be an entrepreneur, involving himself with his capital in the business, or an investor adventuring his money in return for the promise of a share in the profits.

The concept that money itself could be put out to work to earn more money obviously involved a modification of the law of usury. This had already happened. Luther's sense of the potential spiritual benefits of risk and anxiety may have led him to endorse these late medieval amendments to the ancient rule against usury. He emphasised the important distinction between those who lent money at a fixed rate on securities and those who entered into the risk of the borrower, sharing in the prosperous outcome or in the losses incurred.

The principle underlay the joint-stock company. The word

company had a long history before the sixteenth century. It meant literally those who broke bread together (*cum-panis*). One Christian creed spoke of 'the glorious company of the apostles'; soldiers had for long served in companies. The joint-stock company, however, consisted of those who had 'enterprised' (from the French *entre-prendere*, to take in hand) a piece of work, especially one of difficulty, risk or danger. Its members had advanced their capital into the common stock of the trading company in return for a share of the dividend—as the total sum payable as interest on a loan or as the profit of a joint-stock company came to be known by 1623. In the days before limited liability the risks could be considerable: a merchant ship or privateer in distant waters could make its owners a fortune—or sink without trace. So devout Puritans in commerce did not want for occasions which drove them to their knees in humble prayer, as Luther had envisaged.

The Reformers' emphasis on daily work as the means of fulfilling the Christian's calling to serve his neighbour, coupled with their endorsement to the receipt of dividend shares as a payment for risk, attracted earthly returns in full measure to their followers. The Puritan interpreted these material gains as the signs of God's personal interest in him. Therefore the reformed Christian would not spend his profits in Vanity Fair, but rather bestow most of his riches upon the poor and needy, or finance the preaching of the Gospel in all parts of the earth.

THE SECULAR AGE

The new liberty of the Christian man preached by the Reformers and applied in the business sphere by Reformed theologians rested upon the assumption that all men were Christian believers (except infidels and Jews who were beyond the pale of society), living in a universe subject to God's laws, natural and revealed. Luther's picture of vocation also implied the life of the village or small town, where work happened in the context of personal relations. Between 1500 and 1900, however, profound religious and social changes rendered both sets of assumptions largely untrue for many people in the West. Most people were not Christians except in name, nor consciously motivated by a Christ-like desire to give costing service to others. Nor did workers in factory, mill or mine now see the face of the personal neighbour whom Luther had made the moral end of all vocational work.

These changes, neither sudden nor complete, were fed by—and were sources of—the mysterious process we call secularism. Its roots lay deeper than the Renaissance, when a shift of intellectual interest and valuing from the next life of heaven to this world and its pre-occupations showed itself in the work of artists and the writings of Christian humanists. This re-orientation on the part of the intellectual, social and political leaders of Europe moved in concert with a heightened sense of the potential of man. The god-like attributes of creativity and reason of man stood out more boldly than the medieval picture of humanity as imprisoned in a temporary, frail and condemned habitation: his flesh only fodder for the worms and his soul waiting to be pulled to and fro by red-hot demon pincers and the hands of angels.

Secularism enabled such areas as science to establish their independence from the skirts of the 'queen of sciences', theology. Nature's laws could be studied without reference to the authoritative revelations of Church and Bible. Therefore money, commerce and industry could also shake off the old clothes of religion and Jewish-Christian morality. Political economy emerged as the theoretical science of the laws governing the production and distribution of wealth. Adam Smith's survey of the art of managing the resources of a people and its government appeared in 1776, entitled *The Wealth of Nations*. In the following decades his doctrines did much to further the division of labour in industry, a vital strand in the Industrial Revolution. Moreover, he taught that the pursuit of profit would issue naturally in the good of others. Competition and the law of supply and demand would keep prices (and therefore profits) at the lowest point. All moral restraints on the desire for gain could be relaxed. In 1775 Samuel Johnson captured the optimism in the air with a celebrated remark: 'There are few ways in which a man can be more innocently employed than in getting money.'

THE LONG SHADOWS OF CHRISTIAN IDEALS

During the nineteenth century these secular whisperings swelled into the 'melancholy, long-withdrawing roar' of a visibly declining level of Christian faith. But the Reformation counter-thrust lived on in secular forms, even while the outer sandcastles of belief were being toppled one after the other by the combined currents of reason, science and scholarship.

The warm neighbourly love in Luther's vision of the true motive for work changed into the semi-secular ideal of service. Both duty and service flourished in the middle classes, who occupied themselves with land or in the professions: to be in trade retained a certain social stigma. Samuel Smiles, who wrote in 1900 a book called *Duty*, did his best to preach the semi-secular ideals to the men of business. Nelson, the martyr to duty, and Florence Nightingale, heroine of service, were offered to the capitalist owners of England's 'dark, Satanic mills' for their emulation. But on the whole they preferred his earlier gospel of self-help.

Moreover, the entrepreneurs of the late nineteenth century gained comfort from the applications of Darwin's *Origin of Species* (1859) to social and economic life. Nature favoured the survival of the fittest: indeed the whole end of life seemed to be surviving in a hostile and competitive environment. The end justified the means. Samuel Smiles sensed that he was fighting a losing battle. With a voice reminiscent of Amos or Hosea, he could write: 'The spirit of the age is not that of a trader, but of a gambler. The pace is too fast to allow of any one stopping to inquire as to those who have fallen out by the way. They press on; the race for wealth is for the swift. Their faith is in money. It needs no prophet to point out the connection of our distress with the sin of commercial gambling and fraud, and of social extravagance and vanity, of widespread desolation and misery.'

Owing to the growth of populations, technological advances and the factory production methods of the Industrial Revolution, the opportunities for acquiring wealth were now both enormous and open to all social classes in the industrialised countries. Those surviving fragments of the Reformation meteor—duty, service, thrift, character, hard work—all shed their fading lights, but the glint of gold in the unmapped hills of capitalism drew immense human energies inexorably towards them. Outward forms of Christian worship and morality were maintained, indeed amid much religiosity and some fervour. But the steel shutters dividing Sunday from the other six days of the week had fallen into place.

THE AGE OF THE DINOSAURS

By the 1870s and 1880s the Promised Land of the religion of capitalism lay westwards—the United States. Here, Samuel Smiles warned his readers, 'The almighty dollar is the true divinity and its worship is universal.'

Yet moral scruples did not trouble the entrepreneurs who founded the great American corporations: they were too busy. They inherited both a secularised form of Christianity and also the liberating philosophies of Adam Smith and Charles Darwin. John D. Rockefeller, founder of Standard Oil, attributed his vast wealth to the law of the survival of the fittest. He had vanquished competitors because his strength had prevailed over their weakness. His success rested upon the laws of God and nature. Moreover, he had given away 530 million dollars for medical research. Andrew Carnegie, an expounder of the 'duty of a man of wealth', built 3,000 public libraries and gave 7,000 organs to churches. After making his fortune he retired to his native Scotland to give it away. Echoing the spirit of medieval Christendom, though very much a secular man himself, Carnegie declared that 'The man who dies rich, dies disgraced.'

CHAPTER 2

Business and Society

Besides observing at least the outward form of the compromise of a just balance between giving and receiving, the men of business contributed to the medieval social order by being taxed of a large part of their profits, and by giving away another large portion to alleviate such social sufferers as the poor, sick, crippled, widows, and dying. In return both Church and State accorded their merchants and tradesmen honourable places in the social order, signified by minor titles, urban privileges, and special religious places of worship.

The Reformation touched upon the motives of the merchant, but left his place or station in society unaffected. Indeed, it enhanced his status in one important respect. As distinctive nations received the accolade of political independence the function of trade as a method of social intercourse between the 'dis-empired' peoples took on a new importance. In order to barter it was necessary to meet and talk, and the sum of the ensuing personal relationships, based on reciprocal giving and receiving, favoured the maintenance of international peace. Thus trade and peace could be regarded almost as synonyms. As Christians valued peace so they valued the progress of commerce. By contrast, war disrupted trade and exhausted the royal treasure, itself garnered more and more from the nation's profits in commercial competition and interchange with its neighbours.

The essential continuity of the medieval and modern Christian estimate of this major social function of business can be seen, for example, in the writings of Thomas Fuller, a celebrated Anglican divine in the early seventeenth century. In 1642 he wrote of the good merchant as 'One who by his trading claspeth the island to the continent, and one country to another.' This worthy trader neither wrongs the retailers who buy his commodities nor the country's security. 'As for the Commonwealth,' wrote Fuller, 'it far surpasses my skill to give any rules thereof; only this I know, that to export things of necessity, and to bring in foreign needless toys, makes a rich Merchant, and a poor Kingdom . . . ' Behind these words lie the roots of an ancient concern that commerce should practise a form of social responsibility over the urgent matter of defence, which links the early use of merchant ships for war vessels with the much later mercantile system of laws to ensure a supply of military *materiel* in time of need. Besides the contribution to peace and national security, Fuller might also have mentioned the contemporary services of the merchant to society as a dealer in foreign exchange, a minor diplomat, and a postal carrier, all important functions before the evolution of our present intricate consular machinery, postal systems and stock markets.

Fuller emphasised the morality of honest trading with the retailer, which he summed up by citing 'our Saviour's whole-sale rule' of doing to others as you would have them do to you. He doubted not that England had been right to take up cloth-making, for 'The riches of a kingdom does consist in driving the home-commodities thereof as far as they will go, working them to their very perfection, employing more handicrafts thereby.' Significantly he makes no mention of usury: the wholesaler is justified in taking a greater gain because of the care, pains and cost of gathering and distributing his wares, and therefore it was up to retailers to keep prices down—a modern note.

Fuller pointed out that an advantage of England lay in the lack of rigidity in the social structure compared with continental countries: 'The Temple of Honour is bolted against none, who have passed through the Temple of Virtue: nor is a capacity to be gentile denied to our Yeoman, who thus behaves himself.' Yet within months that social structure received a shaking from which it has never quite recovered. For the English Civil War broke out in 1642, the very year that Fuller's book entitled *The Holy State and the Profane State* appeared in print. Indeed the Anglican divine forsook his study and enlisted as military chaplain to the King's General in the West that year.

In the centuries which saw the slow decline of the distinction between holy and profane, the value of the State as such advanced, drawing in its wake the value of commerce as the producer of national wealth and the bond of international peace. An unscrupulous minority of traders may have used the theories of Adam Smith, Ricardo and Malthus to justify their private pursuit of financial profits at the expense of any obligation to society. But the vast respectable majority of manufacturers and merchants slept secure in the conviction that their production, distribution and exchange of goods benefited England, a belief amply justified when trade drew the British Empire in its wake.

In 1642 Fuller wrote of the yeoman of the day as 'a gentleman in ore, whom the next age may see refined'. The development of the middle classes in the following two hundred years amply confirmed his prediction. These new and prosperous middle classes accepted the ermine mantles and liveries of the former merchant princes and also their social duties: customs and taxes for the national wealth, and the missionary work of spreading Christian civilisation from Hudson's Bay to the China Sea.

THE RELIGION OF SOCIETY

The mature Christian attitude to society had betrayed a certain ambivalence: a Yes and No which can be best summed up by the phrase 'in the world but not of it'. The decline of Christian belief weakened the influence of the *negative* pole in this attitude. This erosion left both the natural value of human society and the added value (stemming from the Christian concept of the Kingdom of God) floating in the atmosphere unchallenged. The combination of these values in the post-Christian age gave us the concept of society as a supreme moral end, the goal for human concern and work. Like Mammon it now attracted religious worship as a kind of god.

For example, a religious devotion to man formed the core of Auguste Comte's writings. Significantly Comte is counted among the founding fathers of sociology. This discipline emerged from a marriage between the new quasi-religious value of society and another demi-god of the day, the natural sciences. The infant child, named social sciences, reflected the belief that something called society actually existed, and that it could be studied as an end in itself by scientific methods, not without votive sacrifices of time and money. Persuading the adherents of the long-established god of wealth and their political representatives to finance this infant theology of society at universities proved to be an uphill task. For the historians had entrenched themselves firmly in the universities by the late nineteenth century as the oracles of society, and the political economists stood next in line for recognition as social interpreters.

The sociologists, social anthropologists and social psychologists may now represent the educated theologians of society, but most of us are not intellectuals. For the vast majority of people the rising value of society came in the form of a social ethic. The roots of this social ethic go down on one side to the *pro bono publico* motive of Greece and Rome; on the other, they tap deeply the springs of the Judaeo-Christian religions. In the nineteenth century this moral obligation to serve society came under the umbrella word of duty. In 1880, for example, Samuel Smiles, standing somewhat between Christianity and the fully secular moral spirit of his time, could confidently declare: 'First, there is the pervading abiding sense of duty to God. Then follow others: duty to one's family; duty to our neighbours; duty of masters to servants, and of servants to masters; duty to our fellow-creatures; duty to the State, which also has its duty to perform to the citizen.'

The moral philosophy of Kant undergirded this subjective 'ought' feeling by giving it a certain intellectual respectability.

Meanwhile John Stuart Mill and the Utilitarians argued the case on non-religious rational grounds for making 'the greatest good for the greatest number' the guiding principle of moral conduct. Thus maximising human happiness in society as a whole came to be claimed as the true end of human life. It could also be used as a practical yardstick for the reform of the present social and political institutions, such as prisons. But if the principle applied to prisons, why not to factories and mills as well?

THE INFLUENCE OF SOCIALISM

Sociology also counts Karl Marx among its patriarchs. His thesis rested partly upon the assumption that he had found the missing moral victim of capitalism, the face of the loser whom the Church had apparently ignored as the price for her share in the ill-gotten riches of Mammon. This loser was not an *individual*, for capitalism had become so complex that persons were rarely trading in personal relationships with their village neighbours. The sacrifice on the altar of Mammon was none other than a *class*—the working class throughout the world. The workers had paid the full price by alienation from their village neighbours—and hence the true meaningfulness of work—through the industrial organisation of their labour for private profit. The situation could only be made good when all shared equally the ownership of the means of production and also the surplus profit. As the rich would not disgorge without a fight, the inexorable advance towards the classless society lay through struggle.

For historical reasons the communist gospel of physical revolution lacked support in Britain. The brief baptism of the English Civil War, coupled with a horrified observation of the French 'Terror', did not dispose the middle classes to stand by while the chains of capitalism were violently cast off. Instead socialism developed naturally into the British Labour Movement and achieved after the Second World War certain goals, such as the nationalisation of some major industries. The purpose of socialism in Britain emerged as not so much to abolish capitalism as to

27

reform it in the service of the social end. The socialists wanted to make society morally less evil.

SOCIAL SERVICE AND SOCIAL RESPONSIBILITY

The ideal of service to society as a whole—not to the personally known neighbour—developed in Civil Service, the Imperial Civil Service and the Armed Services. Industry and commerce were counted by the Victorians as outside the pale of patriotic service and the service of needy individuals. Thus trade was not a suitable occupation for gentlemen nor for morally earnest Christians (except the Non-Conformists who were barred from the Universities of Oxford and Cambridge). For service implied putting the interests of some other person or the country before your own, not seeking to add to your interest at their expense.

With the rise of secular society's value in the twentieth century, even those occupations—once the preserve of Christian charity—which helped the needy in a personal way came to be known also as social service. All the old Christian vocations, albeit at different speeds, moved towards a secular stance; the word 'vocation' gave way to the more neutral 'profession' in their brochures. The motive of service, however, with its natural return of high social status and esteem, remained theoretically dominant. Indeed Auguste Comte invented a new word for it, 'altruism' (from the Latin *alteri huic*, 'to this other'). In 1877, for example, he could write of 'the religion of humanity, whose great moral principle is altruism'. It was renamed 'social interest' in the 1930s by the celebrated psychologist Alfred Adler, and became the prime challenger for the crown worn by the profit motive.

The advance of this social motive into the heart of business became practically possible through the emergence of the profession of management. The size and complexity of big business as the nineteenth century progressed led to the recruitment of managers who were not owners or even major shareholders. They were neither fish nor fowl, being intermediaries between capital and labour. Yet the needs of great industrial empires called for more

than mere clerks or administrators: the manager as a leader
needed breadth of vision, intelligence and character. These
attributes were to be found in the middle classes, who happened
to be also the seat of the professions. But the professional ideal
implied not only a knowledge and competence, but also an attitude
of service to others. As heirs to secularised Christianity and reared
in its ethos by the public schools, the British middle class managers
were imbued with a sense of social responsibility. Thus the capitalist entrepreneurs were dragging in a Trojan Horse: a breed of
men different from themselves in some important respects.

Paradoxically the demands of modern war, which did so much to
stimulate the growth of big business and great profits, also educated
several generations of these professional managers in the military
ideals of service and self-sacrifice. Having seen comrades die for
them, these future managers could not return to selfish profit
making. They had a trust to keep, which could only be discharged
by making the world a better place. If the common good of their
country and the quality of human life on earth were worth dying
for, why not live for them?

Many of the slain millions were not fellow officers but common
soldiers, drawn from the industrial slums of the cities, whole
battalions from a single neighbourhood or area. The impression-
able young officers returning after the two World Wars had a
vision of the essential oneness of human nature, and the corresponding superficiality of class barriers. Some were determined that
the comradeship of war would live on in factory and office. The
Armed Services had imbued them with an instinctive leadership,
including the willingness to care for each individual soldier. The
subaltern knew his men by name, buried them with dignity, and
not infrequently visited their bereaved families in their slums
created by the profit motive unchecked. In the trenches and on the
beaches men had found themselves brothers. Could they forget in
prosperity what they had thus learnt in adversity?

The presence of this new sense of the value of society in the
1920s, enshrined in a mushroom growth of business philosophies

and codes of ethics, can be traced in the popularity of such words as 'trusteeship' and 'service' in writings about management. 'Service' described a growing but not uncontested philosophy of the appropriate conscious attitude of business to society. The concept of management as a trusteeship had its roots in the period before the First World War, when the emergence of managers as a professional group had become most obvious. 'Upon these men,' wrote a professor of commerce at Michigan University in 1913, 'will rest a sort of trusteeship to preserve the property intrusted to them, and a demand for leadership to guide and guard their employees . . .' He foresaw 'a new race of executives, which shall justly appreciate the various classes of responsibility resting upon it'. Such were the seeds which flourished in the post-war years before the shadow of the Depression darkened all optimism for a time.

The theme revived after the Second World War. In *Adventure of a White Collar Man* (1941) Alfred P. Sloan interpreted the concept of trusteeship as an almost unlimited challenge for business management to 'expand its horizon of responsibility'. For it 'can no longer confine its activities to the mere production of goods and services. It must consider the impact of its operations on the economy as a whole in relation to the social and economic welfare of the entire community.' The plurality of interests and values entrusted to senior management called for a different kind of leadership than the traditional image of the ruthless entrepreneur. 'Those charged with great industrial responsibility,' wrote Sloan, 'must become industrial statesmen.'

Social responsibility, the concept that the interests of society must be taken into account, could at first co-habit with the continuing dominance of the profit motive. Lip service could be paid to social needs; minor legal restrictions accepted. Above all, the creation of wealth through profit-seeking could be advanced as the chief social contribution of business. But many managers and investors, being middle-class wage earners and not entrepreneurs, found it natural to blend the social motive with their moderately strong profit motive. Thus the absolute supremacy of the profit motive in the minds of managers and shareholders could no longer be taken for granted.

Some managers cautiously began to explore the implication of the service motive in their professional status, and to discuss the possibility of a professional code of ethics. Such tentative moves still assumed that a business enterprise in capitalism must first and foremost be profitable. Social responsibility, whatever its precise meaning, could be accepted as the guarantor of long-term profitability. As the motto of the American Rotary Club in the 1930s summed it up: 'He profits most who serves the best.'

CONCLUSION

Businessmen have generally taken account of the value of society throughout history, if only because the disintegration of social life would spell the death of all commercial and profitable activity. Within a Christian *milieu* they absorbed the high value placed on the common life. The surplus money of trade, taxed in various ways, contributed to the 'common wealth'. Industry and commerce made available to all the goods that the society needed for its security and prosperity, while commercial intercourse promoted its understanding, mutual interdependence and peace with neighbour nation-societies.

Although contemporary business has largely shunned the 'religion of society' as Utopian, it has shown an awareness of the rise in the value of society over against the value of money. We may not now deify society as the supreme end of work and sole source of all morality. Yet we all acknowledge its essential vocation to goodness, despite the many grim parables of cruel and evil societies in history. As both an expression and instrument of society, business is inextricably caught in that upward calling to goodness.

CHAPTER 3

The Individual

The necessity for a separate chapter on the value of the individual person may seem odd. For is not the individual a part of society, and society no more than a collection of individuals?

But the truth is surely more complex than that. In the first place, a society is *more* than the sum of its parts. As a corporate whole it possesses a personality and set of needs of its own. These distinctively social characteristics develop in any human society whatever its particular manifestations: families, crowds, work groups, gangs, tribes, organisations, communities, nations and so on. Of course it is the existence of these 'wholes' which differ from their 'parts' which gives point to such disciplines as social psychology and sociology.

Secondly, the individual may be thought to possess a value quite *distinct* from his membership of a society. Our awareness and recognition of this unique personal value has developed rapidly in recent times, but it has still been overshadowed by the more powerful values of money and society. We might compare it to a tender and fragrant plant in a garden, often starved of food and light but somehow struggling upwards. The word 'individual' contains the story wrapped up in itself. For it used to mean 'indivisible from', so that an 'individual' was essentially united with others. Now, stood on its head, we use the word to express the uniqueness of a person, or that which distinguishes or separates him from the rest. Behind this late semantic change, however, there lies a long history.

The Individual

It could be claimed that it is in the family that the value of the individual has its origin, and there is obvious truth in that. It is the instinct of a mother to value her child, and the child comes to value parents and relatives. In the family values and needs are closely linked. Does the mother value the child because she needs him, or the child love the mother for her food, warmth and affection? Almost certainly she senses a value in her baby which is distinct from her need for him, or his for her. But the valuing of individuals in families retains a flavour of need, even when the children are growing up.

The natural self-centredness of the child at first leads him to value those who respond in some way or another to his value, by meeting his physical needs or by noticing him more than once. Thus a mutual exchange of value takes place. The child's valuing faculty differentiates as it moves away from the centre of self. Cousins have less value than brothers or sisters. And as the valuing faculty scans further outwards its return messages become progressively weaker. People in his village or county are still 'better' than those in the south (or the north). The value placed on foreigners steadily decreases as the distance grows: the less they are like the members of our immediate or tribal family the less value they have. This value-reduction allows men to think thoughts, commit crimes and atrocities involving others which they would regard as intolerable if a member of their own family was the object of them. 'We have learned', wrote the celebrated psychologist Professor C. A. Mace in 1959, 'that the radiant warmth of the human heart varies with the square of the social distance, so to speak.'

INDIVIDUALS IN ANCIENT TIMES

Primitive tribes and ancient empires put much more stress on the social unit than the individual. Yet in Hellenic society the implications of being an individual emerged in literature and drama. The myth of Prometheus, the speeches of Pericles, and the heroes of

Greek tragedy were but three examples of the growing sense of individual existence. Indeed our word 'personality' derives from the Latin word *persona*, a theatrical mask. Socrates comes on the scene as an individual who insisted upon thinking for himself: his refusal to bow his knee to the consensus opinions of society earned him a martyr's death in 399 BC. The Cynics claimed to follow the Socratic tradition by advocating an extreme individualism, where each person exists for himself, society is regarded as an aggregate of individuals and social institutions exist only to serve individuals.

The Bible followed a different way towards the recognition of the value of each individual person. At first the corporate personality of their tribe or of Israel filled the consciousness of the Jewish people. Their tribal god protected and united them; in return Israel attempted to copy the character of the individual deity who had adopted them. This God of Israel, it appeared, wanted moral goodness because he was holy. Unlike Moloch, for example, he did not care for human sacrifice. Israel must keep his moral and social laws. These demands could be tolerated (and had to be met) because this god with the unmentionable name and unique power out-godded all other gods in the vicinity. He was a primitive nuclear deterrent, whose inner laws and nature were imperfectly understood. He would protect those twelve tribes who wore circumcision as the badge of their common faith.

After conquering the Promised Land the tribes of Israel became a settled and prosperous people, far removed from the hungry bedouin wanderers of Sinai. Wealth and relative security, mingled with the fascinations of other gods and religions, exposed the moral concordat with God to constant temptation. The prophets of the eighth century BC spoke out against this 'whoring' after other gods. While feeling a solidarity with their people, these prophets became lonely in their alienation from kith and kin. 'I sat alone,' wrote Jeremiah. Like those of psalmists, his writings showed a self-awareness and introspection of the inner personal life. Jeremiah could not have withstood the rough treatment which came his way, such as solitary confinement in an empty cistern cut in the rock, unless he had been convinced that God must value or care for him as an individual.

Both Jeremiah and Ezekiel supported the emergence of the moral accountability of individuals before God. The punishment of the family or tribe for the sins of some of its members had been common in early times, probably because it was easier to identify and catch up with a group than an individual. It was assumed that God would operate on the same principle. These prophets, however, pointed out that God could see everyone; nobody could hide from him or escape his vengeance. Therefore the sins of each individual would be upon his own head. The sense of the corporate personality of Israel remained strong, but individual responsibility within it took some infant steps forward.

THE CHRISTIAN CONTRIBUTION

The teaching and actions of Jesus revealed an awareness of the value of individual persons. He taught that God numbers the hairs on a man's head; that there is more joy in heaven over one sinner who repents than over ninety-nine people who need no repentance. 'Fear not, therefore, you are of more value than many sparrows.' Nor does God confine his attention to the fold of Israel and its 'lost sheep': Gentiles such as Roman centurions and Syro-Phoenician women are treated as individuals of value.

The offence of Jesus did not lie in his kind of preaching. Such views were already matters for theological discussion, and insofar as they departed from orthodoxy they merited only the punishments which have always been reserved for social or ideological deviants. But the man from Nazareth apparently made such value-judgements not on the basis of the Holy Writings, but on his own authority. Thus by implication he was claiming to be the source of moral values: if he said this was good, it was good; if he said that was evil, then it was evil. This man therefore seemed to be usurping the place of Israel's God, or at least its revered patriarchs. The prophets had prefaced their message with 'Thus saith the Lord'; this man spoke as if he were the Lord.

The Jewish (or Roman) authorities countered by nailing this new 'source of values' to a cross, a crude means of discounting any alternative to *their* national and family system of values. But killing ideas is not easy. Jesus seems to have foreseen his violent death (if not the exact manner of it) and to have prepared for it by gathering twelve disciples—a symbolic number for the twelve tribes of Israel. They became convinced that Jesus did indeed have the value of God. In an individual, despised and rejected by his people and deserted in the hour of need by his friends, God had wrought his work of saving the world.

Into the values of this individual, once the vulnerable carpenter of Nazareth and now the new corporate personality of humanity, each Christian entered by way of baptism. Regardless of race, nation, gender or class, his value as an individual—created in the image of God and re-created by the redemption of Christ—stood solemnly affirmed at the font. Each Christian received a new name to preface his family one, a token that he could follow the saints in closeness to Christ. Ideas do not change reality overnight, but the seeds of individual personal worth had been sown.

When the Christian Church and the Roman Empire joined forces in the fourth century the citizenship of both Rome and the New Jerusalem could be enjoyed by their members. Rome gave the Christian a legal recognition (if he were not a slave) in civic law as a *persona*, accountable in the courts and possessing certain rights and duties. For the value which Rome had placed on its own citizens had been steadily extended—partly as a reward, partly as a bribe—to embrace subject and allied peoples. Membership of the Church guaranteed the value of the person in the eyes of God, and ensured him a share in the divine mercy.

The Roman legal code, it should be noted, extended only to those recognised as citizens, for laws are the rules which maintain order in the circles of tribe and nation. There were plenty of people who did not count as *personae*, both within the Empire and beyond its frontiers, whose fate was a matter of indifference to the authorities, and many of the early Christians had come into this category.

Moreover, Christianity itself could be understood as an earthly value system, with a hierarchy of values for people according to their proximity to Christ: successors to the apostles, saints, martyrs, hermits, those in 'holy orders,' and the laity. But what of the infidel, the apostate or the heretic? The very idea of hell, either as an everlasting torment or an eternal nothingness, implied that there were some individuals upon whom God placed little or no value. If they could be persuaded—or forced—to repent and be baptised, however, their eternal prospects could be dramatically improved.

The evolution from this state of affairs to the position that 'all men, women and children are equal in the sight of God' may be described either as the decline of Christianity or its flowering, again according to the reader's preference. The Reformation paved the way by attacking the whole hierarchical value structure of the medieval Church, declaring the spiritual equality of all Christians regardless of social rank or occupation. Far from being especially valuable individuals, monks were condemned by Luther as useless social liabilities. For him any differences in the Christian Church were entirely ones of function, not of value. Yet Luther in turn confined his vision of true equality to the Christian Church: he did not embrace within it those who rejected the name of Christian, such as the Turks.

THE EFFECTS OF SECULAR CHANGE

Implicit in Judaic and Christian theology had been the germs of the idea that all humanity has value because the Creator made it and 'saw it was good'. Adam had been regarded as a historical figure, thus limiting this natural goodness to his Jewish and Christian descendant families, but the new scholarship of the Renaissance pointed out that the word 'Adam' meant man in Hebrew. Moreover, the artists, writers and inventors of the Renaissance opened up new vistas of human potential. This enhanced value placed on humanity as the container of semi-divine creative and intellectual gifts, in contrast to the medieval stress on fallen human nature and its need for patience to await the fullness of life in Heaven, could be entertained within the Christian frame of reference, as the writings of Erasmus, More and Colet demonstrate. These religious roots of humanism in the Renaissance should always prevent us from regarding Christianity and humanism as enemies.

Later some individuals and schools of thought did sever this enhanced value of the human from any Christian reference by making man (or humanity) into the most divine or supremely valuable object in the universe. The crown of divinity was pressed upon the brow of man. And reason was his holy spirit.

Like all religions, alas, the worship of man has produced its persecutors as well as its martyrs. But, in one of its branches, it led us to the concept that all individuals have an intrinsic value by virtue of the fact that they incarnate a little of the divine substance called humanity.

We owe to the philosopher Immanuel Kant (1724-1803) the classic secular statement of the moral implications of this line of thought. He emphasised the simple but enormously influential distinction between treating a person as a *means* and as an *end*. 'Act so as to treat humanity never only as means but also as an end,' sums up his philosophical message at this point. These words, destined to be the slogan for the liberal and democratic movements of the following two centuries, deserve careful thought.

Kant developed the concept of a kingdom of ends, in which all members treated each other as ends as well as means. He insisted that we *ought* to act that way, even though we knew that not all our fellow-beings held the same belief or adhered to a similar practice; for example, we *ought* not to cheat because others cheated us, or might be expected to do so.

But why should we behave this way? Kant takes us back to the realm of motive and the nature of goodness as an 'end' in itself if it is to be truly good. Goodness resides in the *good will*, not in such results as success or happiness. He denied any moral merit to actions which are not morally motivated—a hard saying for some businessmen of his day. It was not the consequences which made an action good, but the spirit of intent. In other words, Kant sought to distinguish morality from mere prudence. He also attempted to ground it in the universal experience of man, not in revealed religion. Religion now took second place to morality. You should be religious in order to be good, not moral in order to be on the right footing with God. Many Victorians readily accepted this message.

The philosophy of Kant rested on the existence of a 'categorical' (genuinely moral) imperative for doing things, alongside the 'hypothetical' one, which derives from considering the consequences of actions. The hypothetical thinking concerned means; but the categorical or moral imperative dealt with ends, and must therefore be heeded first. Kant also drove a wedge between values and needs. The moral 'ought' must lead you to act regardless of the consequences in terms of your needs. Always prefer duty to desire.

The influence of Kantian thought on the nineteenth century has already been glimpsed in the elevation of duty. It furthered also the move towards seeing Christianity as raw material for a universal morality of humanity. Yet the Kantian philosophy, like the Christian gospel, could be debased into the notion of treating others as ends in order that they will regard you as an end. Still, it gave new life to the idea that moral goodness really matters. If Kant established the autonomy of morality from theology and metaphysics, he also partially wrested it from the Utilitarians, who believed in assessing actions primarily in terms of consequences. Indeed, for others with eyes to see, his principle may also have come as a reminder of the original Christian gospel of locating goodness in the attitude and motive of giving more, bestowing generous service without thought of a profitable consequence.

Kant's morality rested on the assumption that the individual had value as an end and not only as a means, and that goodness lay in treating him as such regardless of other considerations. His philosophy provided a basis for a compromise between a post-Reformation Christianity sapped by secularism and assaulted by scientism, and the heirs of the Renaissance and Enlightenment. The common front of these forces resulted in the immense energies and great achievements of the humanitarians. Such time-honoured institutions as slavery, prisons and the army received their full attention. Nor could the factories and mills for long escape the reforming zeal of those who insisted that individuals and humanity in any shape or form should be treated as ends as well as means. Their value as members of the human race gave them such a right. The conviction of the absolute nature of their moral motive—the duty which inspired them—led the reformers to dismiss the counter-arguments that dire social consequences would ensue if they dared to change anything.

The humanitarians came into inevitable conflict with those who made Mammon their chief end and regarded people primarily as means to production. They were also sometimes up against those who placed supreme value on society more than the individual as such. For the 'greatest happiness for the greatest number', the doctrine of Jeremy Bentham and John Stuart Mill, could be used as a reply to those who advocated the moral treatment of individuals regardless of the consequences. Therefore, despite some notable individual victories, the progress of the humanitarian movement was very slow throughout the nineteenth and early twentieth centuries.

Eventually, however, the Kantian-Christian-Humanist springtide linked up with other rivers and streams, jointly flowing into the estuary of our present consciousness. Descartes contributed to the definition of man by his dictum *cogito ergo sum*, 'I think therefore I am', which could be interpreted as a foundation for individualism. The Romantic movement, for example, contributed its own concept of heightened individuality as valuable in itself: to be different somehow acquired a value, even if you were bad like Lord Byron or monstrous like Napoleon. The theory of

The Individual

evolution emphasised survival of the fittest individuals among us. Kierkegaard, with his own agonised self-exploration and sense of freedom in decision, and Nietzsche exulting in the uniqueness of every person, were early leaders of the existentialist movement's search for 'authentic selfhood'. Freud's teachings appeared to open up a chasm between the individual and his parents; beneath the façade of family love lay intolerable tensions and conflicts. Yet the value of individuals justified long hours of psycho-analysis to help them to reach full freedom and autonomy, ridding them from socially-inculcated guilt.

The exalted value of the individual created another new theology, called psychology. A life-long study of the mental functions and behaviour of the human individual may have struck our more distant forefathers as being exceedingly strange, for their value system did not give the individual such a pride of place. They were less interested in studying the individual as such, still less what we now call individuality. Later, the prevailing influence of the dominant physical sciences truncated psychology into a shape which passed for a science in academic circles, but in its popular forms it retains the function of a philosophy aimed at the fulfilment of the individual by the individual.

At the centre of the new theology lay the concept of self-realisation, a phrase invented in 1876 to mean the fulfilment by one's own efforts of the possibilities of development of the self. Perhaps the self-scrutiny of the Romantics, like Byron, and the self-help of the practical British were both altar steps leading to this new god of self. The movement's philosophy of individualism emphasised that we must be as free as possible to pursue our own different and unique destinies. Morality merely defined the social limits within which each could seek the goal of self-fulfilment. Humans, imbued with their holy spirit of reason, could be trusted to exercise a temperance which would plainly enhance all their pleasures and dispel selfishness. The words of Alexander Pope summed up the new humanist theology:

The Individual

Know then thyself, presume not God to scan;
The proper study of mankind is man . . .
Two principles in human nature reign;
Self-love to urge, and reason to restrain;
Nor this a good, nor that a bad, we call;
Each works its end, to move or govern all.

One hero of the new individualism was that self-help character of our childhood, Alexander Selkirk alias Robinson Crusoe. Although Defoe portrayed him in *Robinson Crusoe* (1719) as a Christian man, humbly dependent upon God's providence, we think of him as the supreme individualist, displaying ingenuity and creative talent in a desperate situation. Also we sense the other side of the coin of individualism in Crusoe: an awful feeling of cosmic and personal loneliness. William Cowper identified each of us with Robinson Crusoe. His poem 'The Solitude of Alexander Selkirk' opens with the proud and boastful lines:

I am monarch of all I survey;
My right there is none to dispute;
From the centre all round to the sea
I am lord of the fowl and the brute.

But the mood changes abruptly, and we feel the isolation of Selkirk the individual:

I am out of humanity's reach,
I must finish my journey alone.

How the individual could regain the lost 'Society, Friendship, and Love' in an atomised society where tradition, social solidarity and authority have bowed their knees to the god of self becomes a major problem. Perhaps we can take comfort from Crusoe's discovery that he was not alone: in his green tropical island, teeming with fruit and game, he found another individual—a black pagan whom he called Man Friday. Perhaps that aspect of his story has a particular moral for us.

The Individual

The increased sense of the value of the individual person as an end in himself made especially slow headway in manufacturing industry where by necessity people came to be regarded primarily as means to ends, signified by such terms as 'hands' or 'labour' rather than as persons or people. Yet it contributed directly to the humanitarian reforms directed at alleviating the hardships of the Industrial Revolution. Later, humanitarians and Non-Conformists armed with socialist theories, spearheaded the rise of the trade union movement. In essence, these trade unions came into existence to protect the individual worker against exploitation as merely a means to production. At the heart of its message lay the belief that all individuals, regardless of class or station, have a moral right to be regarded as ends as well as means. Therefore each individual's interests within industry should be taken into account.

This fundamental concern for the individual rode on the back of the more powerfully ascendant value of society. The active consideration of the individual had to be promoted under the general aegis of social reform. Mainly for reasons of necessity, backed by Christian and socialist emphases on the collective as opposed to the individual value, the trade union movement presented itself as the champion of a down-trodden *class*, rather than of the *individual* as such. But the distinction cannot be pressed too far. For the working class personified the individual, just as individuals such as the Tolpuddle Martyrs represented the working class. Devout trade unionists hailed each other as 'brothers', a sect within the new religion of Man. They could not afford the aristocratic luxury of full individualist philosophy. Democratic majority rule had to be accepted by the minority. The weakness of political individualism (or anarchy) certainly could not be accepted in the struggle against capitalism proper. Yet the hope of individualism remained: a classless society peopled by a 'new man who will harmoniously combine spiritual and moral purity and a perfect physique' (Programme of the XXII Congress of the Communist Party of the Soviet Union).

The Individual

After the First World War the cause of the individual in industry received new support from the social science faculties of the universities and business schools. At first they came as missionaries of the idea that the corporate life of factories and (large) organisations could become the substitutes of the Church. Just as Bruce Barton in *The Man Nobody Knows* (1925) painted Jesus as the greatest businessman of all time, so the social scientists hailed the Hawthorne findings as the discovery of a new Church on the factory floor. For Professor Elton Mayo and his disciples had finally established the importance to workers of social life and acceptance in the Hawthorne plant of the General Electric Company in Chicago during the late 1920s and 1930s. In *The Social Problems of an Industrial Civilization* (1933), Mayo claimed that his discovery of the group, with its own sense of social responsibility, had revealed the utter inadequacy of individualism, the 'rabble hypothesis' of society which rested, in his opinion, on these main assumptions:

1. Natural society consists of a horde of unorganised individuals.
2. Every individual acts in a manner calculated to secure his self-preservation or self-interest.
3. Every individual thinks logically, to the best of his ability, in the service of this aim.

Mayo confidently believed that these postulates would be replaced by an awareness that workers formed themselves into groups, with appropriate customs, duties, routines, even rituals; and management succeeds or fails insofar as its authority is accepted by the group. Participation in seminars on 'Group Dynamics', known also as 'T-Groups' (Training Groups), was advanced as the only method for initiating or baptising people into the new salvation of social 'belongingness'. In such 'Group Laboratories' a whole generation of managers explored and experienced the power of groups.

The Individual

The extremists which any religion attracts neither had compunction in preaching that groups should pressurise individuals into conformity, nor in advocating the supremacy of reaching group consensus as the only moral method of decision-making. In particular they concentrated upon dispelling the notion of a leader as someone *better* than the group, or unique in any way. Nor were they unnerved by the effective use made by the Chinese in the Korean War of group dynamics as a method of causing mental breakdowns in American prisoners. The assumption that the group would always be morally wiser as well as stronger than the individual was accepted as an unquestioned axiom.

A series of attacks on the orthodoxy of the new religion of groups heralded the return of individualism. Perhaps the chief credit for radically questioning these assumptions belongs to William H. Whyte Jnr. in his seminal book *The Organization Man* (1955). Whyte pointed out that the current concept of the business organisation in America demanded from the manager a particular kind of social ethic which seemed to conflict with his personal ethic. The social ethic has three major propositions: 'a belief in the group as the source of creativity; a belief in "belongingness" as the ultimate need of the individual; and a belief in the application of science to achieve the belongingness.' This social ethic had replaced what he called the 'Protestant Ethic,' which once enhanced individual risk, effort and independence. It not only required people to work for an organisation, but also to *belong* to it like a religion. This social ethic 'rationalises the organisation's demands for fealty' and makes 'morally legitimate the pressures of society against the individual.' Thus William Whyte sounded an alarm bell by his vision of the organisation as the 'Animal Farm' of democracy.

The counter-attack against the dominance of the social scientists secured its intellectual flank by an appeal to the writings of A. H. Maslow, an American professor of psychology who died in 1970. Maslow advocated self-realisation under the new name of self-actualisation, and he pressed morality, religion and mysticism into its service. The Renaissance tradition of man's god-like potential for creativity and goodness lies behind the pages of his psychological monographs. The true moral philosophy of enlightened humanism could be established by studying the lives of its 'saints', the handful of 'self-actualisers' whom Maslow identified among friends, students and historical individuals such as Eleanor Roosevelt. Maslow declared that scientific humanism and religion could once more join forces in the enjoyment, pursuit and study of maximum self-actualisation. Like others before him, he dreamed of a utopia (which he called Eupsycha) peopled by a thousand god-like self-actualisers.

Among the pioneers who paved the way for Maslow's message into industry and commerce in the 1950s and 1960s stands pre-eminent the name of Douglas McGregor, Professor at the Massachusetts Institute of Technology until his death in 1962. In his enormously influential book *The Human Side of Enterprise* (1960), McGregor polarised two sets of assumptions about human nature into the columns of propositions, which he called Theory X and Theory Y. The former contained a mixture of attitudes and views which signified a low estimate of human nature. But Theory Y served as a manifesto for militant humanist reform. It included the proposition that: 'Commitment to objectives is a function of the rewards associated with their achievement. The most significant of such rewards, e.g. the satisfaction of ego and self-actualisation needs, can be direct products of effort directed towards organisational objectives.'

This confidence that self-actualisation can be harmonised with corporate goals presided over the writings of the school which—divested of the 'human relations' and 'social scientists' tags—is now called the behavioural sciences. The much greater emphasis on the value of the individual, smuggled in under the covers of both the common task and the social ethic, is epitomised by the writings of Professor Frederick Herzberg. These can be considered under the general heading of job enrichment, which—with management by objectives—is a contemporary outcome of the work of this school.

The Individual

Professor Herzberg shared to the full the enlightened secular humanism of Maslow; he unhesitatingly put the value of the individual in sovereign position. But he added the gospel of relevance to industry through his researches into the job satisfaction of 203 engineers and accountants in Pittsburgh during the mid-1950s. This empirical or scientific research, later repeated with other kinds of employees, he claimed had proved his theory that intrinsic factors in jobs provided satisfactions for individuals which lasted longer than the effects of the extrinsic (or 'hygiene') factors present.

Behind Herzberg's theory and researches lay a host of value judgements, historical interpretations and plain myths which he published in 1966 under the title of *Work and the Nature of Man*. Herzberg's faith rested upon man's innate potentiality: 'This article of psychological faith gives purpose to man's existence.' Man's destiny is to grow by his own efforts into his full potential. Jung, Adler and Maslow had all glimpsed this goal, but all had failed to define self-actualisation or psychological growth. It is not fear of sin and punishment which constitutes man's primary motivation but his compelling urge to realise his potential as a creative and unique individual, according to his own innate abilities and within the limits of reality, and this end he can achieve by a process of continuous psychological growth.

In contrast to Maslow, Herzberg related his discussion of the characteristics of psychological growth specifically to job capability and performance. Prominent in his list of these attributes comes *creativity*, which is significantly given a very wide definition as 'any knowledge, understanding or principle that originates from the individual'. Herzberg mentions that the term 'insight' is sometimes used to convey this 'non-original' creativity by the individual. Although a concept may be common knowledge by insight he makes it his own, and therefore he has grown.

Within Herzberg's general understanding of growth the realisation of potential creativity means using to the full the manufacturing

47

abilities of people. Therefore jobs should include assignments which do not have built-in solutions or responses. 'Some people are determined; some are determiners. The determiners use their brains for dynamic, creative ability, while the determined are unable to do so.'

Herzberg also lists as a characteristic of growth what he calls *individuation*, the process of becoming an individual. He implies that in America the complementary process of socialisation has tended to swamp the area of individual response to life, a trend which is nothing less than 'partial suicide'. This point is illustrated by the way that personal identity is usually established by reference to membership of groups, e.g. 'I am an engineer' or 'I am a husband'. Herzberg regarded becoming an individual as one of 'the highest levels of psychological growth'. Working with others should not only produce results for that 'fictitious entity' the group, but also provide means for personal enhancement.

The newer emphasis upon the value of the individual stemming from such writings led to the contemporary interest in schemes for promoting job satisfaction by means of job 'enrichment' or 'restructuring'. Such changes, however, had to be justified to management as being consistent with profit-making, at least in the long term. There are signs of progress. In 1973, for example, two Swedish car manufacturers, Volvo and Saab, experimented with changes in the assembly line method in order to promote greater individual work satisfaction and continued high production.

Meanwhile another strand of the behavioural scientists—the industrial sociologists—confused the issue by questioning whether or not the 'job enrichers' were not simply seeking to impose middle-class attitudes to employment upon a deeply-ingrained working-class mentality. The study by the British sociologist J. Goldthorpe of *The Affluent Worker* (1968) suggested that workers took a primarily 'instrumental' attitude to work, treating it as a means to more money for leisure pursuits and not mainly as an end in itself. Thus the 200 Luton factory workers in the research study portrayed no overt desire for 'self-actualising' work. They were interested in the pay packet, and not involved in their work in a vocational way.

Goldthorpe's book came as a timely reminder of the abiding influence of society (in the form of social class) on the attitudes of individuals, both to himself and to his work. The middle classes, including its social scientists, inherited attitudes and concepts which stood at only a few secular removes from Christian values. Moreover, the Christian ethic had imperfectly passed on elements within itself of an older Graeco-Roman humanism, which saw work as the creative exercise of human energy in response to the eternal values of goodness, truth and beauty. These assumptions naturally favoured intellectual and artistic (or creative) forms of work, rather than industrial manufacture.

The enthusiasm of the trade unions for job enrichment has been so far muted. The major reason for this reluctance to seize what may seem to be an obvious banner is that the strategic gaze of the trade union leaders has remained firmly fixed upon the satisfaction of the more basic of human needs of the individual: money (for food, warmth and shelter) and security, especially for job security or the right to work.

In 1972 unemployment in the United Kingdom touched the one million mark. The trade union movement, spearheaded by the Clyde shipyard workers, campaigned on the slogan: 'The Right to Work'. Does the individual have a right to work? On moral grounds the answer is Yes. For the individual has value as an end and work is essential for his well-being.

No particular individual employer (and a company is an individual person at law) has at present the corresponding legal obligation to employ him. Both capitalists and work people have traditionally turned to society as a whole, or its trustees in the government of the day, to find employment for those who find themselves without work or made redundant. From the moral point of view, a society (and economic system) which conversely proved unwilling or unable to find employment for able-bodied people would stand discredited. Nor can that employment ever

49

again be the monotonous drudgery of bygone days: it must be work appropriate to the dignity of an individual person.

CONCLUSION

We may not adopt individualism as a philosophy, or take the actualisation of the self's potential to be the chief end of living, but we share a common belief in the special value of each person and we accord the right to everyone to be treated in common work as a means who remains also an end. Thus each employee has a personal value and a legitimate self-interest and self-love. To care for the quality of life in each employee is therefore to acknowledge and serve a value which reflects—without trapping—the very light of goodness as we are capable of perceiving it.

CHAPTER 4

The Natural Environment

Our contemporary concern for the effects of industry on the environment suggests that another value has emerged from its chrysalis in history. It is the value of nature. As in the case of the individual person, this value comes to us partly disguised in clothes borrowed from society, a much more established and dominant end. For example, the killing of rare animals for furs has largely been condemned not so much because it is intrinsically wrong, but more because society dislikes it. The living world of nature, however, has value entirely of its own. Perhaps only by understanding the history of man's awareness of this value can we appreciate fully the place it merits in our practical decision-making today.

THE BIBLICAL VIEW OF NATURE

The Jews of the Old Testament period appreciated the value of nature in much the same general manner, we may surmise, as did their primitive forefathers and their contemporaries. For nature above all supplied a variety of foods. In addition it provided the means for warmth, and the raw materials for meeting many of the other human needs, such as security, for rocks made possible city walls and bronze and iron could be fashioned into weapons. Man's dependence upon nature may have been more immediate— and therefore more conscious—than it is for us; indeed an awareness of the significance of this living environment pervades the writings of the Old Testament.

In all primitive societies, including early Greece and Rome, the vivid sense of nature merged with religious ideas, especially with various forms of animism, the attribution of conscious life to nature or natural objects. But in Hebrew religion, the faith which influenced our civilisation mainly by way of Christianity, the age-old fusion of man's awareness of the natural environment with his spiritual awareness, took a different line in its development. The Jews believed that a one Maker of all things, the God of Abraham and Isaac, in originally creating the whole universe, including man, had thereby infused all with value according to its kind and degree: 'He saw that it was good,' as Genesis declared.

Man's position within the world could be compared to that of a gardener, a steward entrusted with some one else's valued property. The early offer of animals, wine and fruits in sacrifice signified outwardly this sense that the universe belonged to a creator who delighted in it, a craftsman rejoicing in the work of his hands. The labour of man consisted in working within nature, as part of its economy. (The word 'economy' here has primarily a theological sense. Coming from the Greek term for household management, it was applied at an early date to mean the divine government of the world.) Being unlike any other creature made in the image of God, man could also share delightfully in the great Craftsman's understanding and joy at his handiwork.

The Old Testament thinkers, however, had some difficult questions to answer. Moral evil abounded: men cheated, murdered, lied, and robbed their neighbours. The relations between nations, tribes and even the two sexes did not reflect the picture or interpretation of their theology of an 'economy' of moral goodness. Moreover, physical evils prevailed: animals and birds ate each other, drought and famine hovered, disease of mind and body struck like an arrow in the night, while at the last worms ate man's physical body in the grave. How could all these ills be reconciled with the creation of a good universe by a good God?

Various theories were advanced and held in plurality. Man's endless toil in the stony fields of Palestine and woman's suffering and death in childbirth could be explained as a punishment for an act of disobedience in the first days, when Adam and Eve had fallen for the temptation, mediated by a lower creature, to take from nature what had not been put in it for them. Another theory traced a relation of cause-and-effect between infringements of God's moral law and physical suffering. The incompleteness of the notion of individual accountability allowed a corporate or social understanding to undergird this doctrine. One man's moral sin is another man's physical blindness. As the Hebrew proverb succinctly put it: 'The fathers have eaten sour grapes, and the children's teeth are set on edge.' A third theory, already present if not exactly popular in ancient Israel, is recorded by the Psalmist thus: 'The fool hath said in his heart, There is no God.'

THE CHRISTIAN CONTRIBUTION

The attitude of Jesus to nature, as portrayed in the gospels, is entirely consistent with the basic biblical belief that man, God and nature are indissolubly bound up together in a covenant or contract. God clothes the lilies of the field, he cares for the sparrows which men sell for a few farthings. Part of the mystery of Jesus, however, lay in his apparent lordship over nature. 'What manner of man is this, that even the winds and waves obey him?' The gospels portray him as being in league with nature, both respecting its laws and exerting dominance over it. At his death, we are told, even nature went into mourning: 'and darkness covered the face of the earth'.

Paul also thought within the same Hebraic scheme of things. He imagines nature bound up with man in a common destiny: 'I consider that the sufferings of this present time are not worth comparing with the glory that is to be revealed to us. For the creation waits with eager longing for the revealing of the sons of God; for the creation was subjected to futility, not of its own will but by the will of him who subjected it in hope; because the creation itself will be set free from its bondage to decay and obtain the glorious liberty of the children of God.' But the hope of a dramatic act of re-creation by God's Son descending in glory slowly faded. The whole created universe including its mortal and vulnerable humans, it seemed, had to continue 'groaning in travail' together.

This gradual Christian change of gaze from forwards at a re-fashioned earth—a universe 'made good'—to upwards at a heavenly 'country far beyond the skies' influenced the Christian evaluation of nature. The Christian no longer felt at home within the unredeemed natural order. At least he had experienced the first fruits of promised changes by an inward transformation of his spirit by the Holy Spirit. Having sipped water at the well of eternal life, his eyes were open to the painful imperfections of nature: its cruelty and frustration, its senseless tragedies and alienation from God. A gulf between re-created man and the old creation began to widen.

Moreover, the Christian Fathers reflected upon the fact that the yet unredeemed natural creation proved to be a source of moral and spiritual trials for the 'newborn' men and women of the Lord. Instead of lying down with the lambs, as Isaiah had foretold, the lions could be used to tear Christians to pieces in the Roman arena. Just as the serpent in Eden had been the mouthpiece of moral evil, so the Devil pressed nature into his service against the new life of Christ in man. Above all the physical body of man, still biologically programmed after the old order to seek its own pleasures, stood as a hostage in the enemy's camp. To reject and hate the present natural order, including the body's cry for sex and food, while awaiting in holy patience the coming of the New World, became one ideal in Christianity.

But another basic attitude to nature, implicit in the words of St. Paul quoted above, can be traced to its roots in Christian soil. We can best call it sympathy or compassion. A tender pity for the created order, especially for those creatures who had *anima* (or breath of life) like man, made its presence felt in the Christian mind. It was destined to flower in the life of St. Francis of Assisi. His kindred sympathy for all birds and beasts is celebrated. It included a compassion for the human body. On his death bed in

1226, for example, St. Francis could ask forgiveness from that 'poor brother donkey, my body' for the hardships he had inflicted upon it.

The legends around the name of St. Francis remind us that this sympathy for a universe dumbly waiting its turn for God's re-creation prefaced a new human power to change nature. For Christians were supposed to share in the spirit of Christ, who had once himself exercised a lordship of creator-power while yet in the flesh. Although it is not a dominant theme in the New Testament, such apostles as Paul and Peter were described as employing on occasions a power to influence the creatures of this present 'groaning' universe. Thus nature still acknowledged grudgingly the authority of the Christ-spirit in man. Both the apostles, for example, possessed a gift for healing. St. Paul was unaffected although a viper fastened its jaws into his hands; the fury of storms at sea could not prevail against him. St. Francis shook the paw of a ferocious wolf who had accepted his offer of regular meals in return for leaving alone the townsfolk of Gubbio. Behind these tales lies a deep sense that Christian man could yet bring a limited creative power to bear upon nature and its denizens, by virtue of being the eldest brother in the family of the universe.

In a way this attitude had cut loose from a Hebraic interpretation of life, which held that both people and nature more-or-less received their just desserts. According to this picture, people could save themselves by accepting the moral authority of God and his Law, by entering the Ark of Israel by circumcision or at least by grasping the life-lines thrown out from it to a drowning gentile world. As for nature, the Jews thought that its corruption and 'unclean' aspects had to be separated from its wholesome parts by the application of a rigorous ritual code. By contrast Christians in the lineage of St. Francis saw the natural order, its animals and birds, as already in the same boat with themselves, eagerly awaiting God's promised new creation, and already recognising the divine compassion and power in the works of the Church as pioneer of the Kingdom of Heaven. The leprous beggar, the mentally possessed or the prostitute were brothers and sisters with heavier loads, staggering under the general weight of this unredeemed world, 'subjected to futility, not of its own will but by the will of him who subjected it in hope'.

THE DECLINE OF CHRISTIAN FAITH

Doubtless the reader will by now not be surprised by the fate of the value of nature during these centuries when the Christian faith entered a twilight period as a credible intellectual system. Both the opposing tendencies latent in Christianity—to see nature as increasingly different from man and to see it as spiritually close to us—steadily developed while at the same time their explicit Christian framework of ideas was falling away into the background like a spent rocket casing.

The tendency towards kinship culminated in the worship of nature as a supreme value, the true god of man. This new and divine source of 'perpetual benediction' found its most ardent spokesman in the English poet William Wordsworth. Not only had nature assumed the aura of God, it had also taken over the moral functions of Christian religion. The nature lover could read 'sermons in stones'. The Bible of nature could restore the wounded spirit by revealing what is right and wrong better than any human preacher:

> One impulse from a vernal wood
> May teach you more of man,
> Of moral evil and of good
> Than all the sages can.
>
> Sweet is the love which Nature brings;
> Our meddling intellect
> Mis-shapes the beauteous forms of things:
> We murder to dissect.

This note of morality in Wordsworth's poetry sets him apart from many of the later apostles of pantheism. Sensing himself to be 'Nature's priest', Wordsworth conceived it to be his vocation to live in the Lake District, that natural temple in whose inner misty sanctuary as a boy he once glimpsed the 'vision splendid' of an earth 'apparelled in celestrial light'. But Wordsworth felt that man as a whole was called to be that 'happy warrior', who is 'doomed to go in company with pain, and fear, and bloodshed' yet in face of them exercising a power which 'controls them and subdues, transmutes, bereaves of their bad influence, and their good receives'. It is not difficult to hear an echo of that Christian tradition, so imaginatively epitomised but not exhausted by the life of St. Francis of Assisi, that man should be involved in nature and in the alleviation of creaturely needs.

The moral aspect of nature, which both secular humanists and Christians accepted in varying degrees, took a savage knock in the writings of the Darwinian school of evolutionists. In one sense the god nature gained more prominence as the old God of the Bible was pushed back further beyond the supposed year of creation 4004 BC into the limbo of time as a First Cause. But nature lost its place as a higher authority than man. Far from favouring goodness nature, as now revealed, reserved her favours for the strong and fit.

Indeed to some Victorian sensibilities the scientific or objective study of nature had disclosed not a god but a demon, a Moloch thriving on human suffering. The shock to Victorian religious belief was deep and protracted. The Marquis de Sade had already jumped the gun in 1792: 'Nature averse to crime? I tell you that nature lives and breathes by it, hungers at all her pores for bloodshed, yearns with all her heart for the furtherance of cruelty.' Thus nature, still personified as a blind divinity or life-force, could be seen as essentially evil in the old human categories. But if nature *was* evil, then evil was the same as goodness. For nature was the supreme whole, the source and end of all things. Thus man would be most natural (i.e. good) when he lived up to the new ethic of nature, which he had once—under the influence of biblical myths —called 'evil'.

For those who remained Christian the revelation that nature

was either amoral or downright immoral strengthened enormously the ancient option of revulsion from it and from all natural functions, as being completely alien or hostile to Christian man (alias enlightened man, alias civilised man). Clearly the whole of nature lay outside the sphere of morals, and therefore man had no moral obligation to nature or his body. He had merely to respect nature as a strong and ruthless force, and master its brute energies. But the implicit sense of kinship, the leaping hope that creation would praise its Maker, the compassionate response to all its lame ducks, the reverence for 'all things bright and beautiful' as channels of communication between a moral creator and his human vice-regents: all had gone, swept away it seemed for ever, down the drain of history.

THE RE-DISCOVERY OF NATURE

Traditionally, practical men of business have always regarded their natural surroundings as mines of potential raw materials waiting to be turned into wealth. Such abstract notions as 'nature' or the 'environment' have invaded the boardroom very recently, and then partly disguised—as already noted—in the clothes of the much more established and wider-embracing value of society. The acceptance of the general ideas that business exists to serve society, and that a commercial organisation is (or should be) a microcosm of society at large, has already led the councils of industry to be much more sensitive to the value-shift among peoples throughout the world to the natural environment.

The streams which have flowed into this new awareness of the value of the natural environment in business, and its muted moral claim to be treated as an end and not just as a means, are many and confused. Yet some rivulets may be mapped. Obviously there is the widespread anxiety based upon our human need for security, safety and survival. Fear that natural resources will be exhausted by the voracious appetite of industry serving a world population of some 3,500 millions which grows annually by leaps and bounds, has led to a universal interest in conservation. Fear that bad health and even mass homicide will result as industrial effluents poison or foul the atmosphere has added to the drive for the conservation of nature, the movement against pollution in all its forms: smells, tastes and noise.

Merging with these fast-running streams are the waters of another river, the one whose earlier course in its long historical reaches has already been outlined in this chapter. At its centre runs like an invisible current the more positive Franciscan sense of nature, but in a secularised form which does justice to the Darwinian revolution. The use of natural science to prove or disprove the existence of God has indeed died away, but a certain wonder and delight in creation, mixed with religious awe at its vast size, persists. If the moral goodness of nature has departed, so also has the equally religious idea of its evil or cruel properties. The belated recognition of nature as amoral, moreover, has served to increase man's awareness that he is the only known moral agent in the universe. He finds himself morally responsible for the fate of bird, beast and fish: indeed for the whole created universe within his reach.

In company with this change in moral sensibility has come a new sense of affinity with nature, a growth in the feeling of involvement or one-ness at the expense of the rejection of all that savours of animalism and the maintaining of a formal distance between the orders of creation and redemption. The writings of modern zoologists, professional and amateur, have emphasised patterns of behaviour in animals which resemble us or remind us of ourselves. Through popular books and television programmes their message has reached a mass audience, who in daily life are none other than the familiar consumers, customers, employers and employees of industry.

Naturalists in the mould of Darwin the patriarch gave way to the theologians of nature, who in turn were replaced by their secular counterparts, the ecologists. Significantly the word ecology derives from the same Greek root word as economy (*oikos*, house), and it centres upon the study of the mutual relations between organisms and their environment. The ecologists have already shown us how much nature works a *system*, each part performing a useful function. Thus it has a claim to be regarded and treated as a whole; to damage or destroy one part is to threaten the viability of the whole.

There are even Franciscan notes of a new sense of compassion, as told in Joy Adamson's book and film *Born Free* (1960). The story of a woman's maternal care for orphaned lion cubs clearly touched a vibrant cord in the human heart. Tales of man's power to understand and enter into empathy with wild animals and regions abound. Even wolves disclose to the loving and patient human eye an inner world of family relationships and playful affection which would have delighted St. Francis. Above all, we experience the distinctive vocation which comes to us when we see nature in disarray, or speaking to us through its needs and mute questions. Not in sermons but through such wordless eloquence nature still connects with the morality in man.

Behind the nineteenth century pastime of shooting wild life lay the dark philosophy that wild beasts exhibited the cunning and cruelty of the hopeless and unregenerate animal kingdom. Being totally alien from the kingdom of man, the wild creatures were fit only for slaughter for food or sport, or if they so much as raised a paw against man or his enslaved beasts. 'Wild' is synonymous with 'cruel' and 'evil'. Thus wild animals were 'fair game': being immoral they provoked man's righteous moral reaction of extermination. Even today fox hunters occasionally advance the 'cruelty' of foxes wantonly snapping heads of hens as a moral justification for the sport.

This moral reaction to an immoral nature extended to some peoples. Savages such as Red Indians or African natives were grouped with animals in the same order or system, on account of their cruelty, and so they also could be slaughtered without pity when occasion demanded it. Such half-people were disturbing reminders of man's own cruel and evil past in the coils of evolution, before he had raised himself by reason and science to the prosperous civilisation of the West. Now, however, we recall the fate of the American Red Indian at the hands of our fathers' fathers with a deeper compassion and guilt, much as we mourn the passing of the great buffalo herds. 'Buffalo Bill', slayer of both buffalo and Indians, would be surprised at his present infamy.

It is possible that the male attitude to woman has been influenced by the prevailing value-perception of nature. In both Hellenic and biblical civilisations, men traditionally regarded women as being closer to nature in spirit than men. This view survived both the balancing impact of the Christian message, and the exaggerated counter-view of later centuries that woman was naturally a superior moral being to man. We may note the persistence of boring, monotonous and sub-human toil by women in industry. The old agrarian belief that the hard labour of the fields is fit work for beasts, women and tamed savages or slaves has its counterpart in contemporary life. Some women feel that they are the last of the trilogy to attain to emancipation. Certainly many more feel that their values as members of human society and as individuals in their own right are not appreciated by men. Such a conviction has already influenced British industry and commerce in this decade by the gradual introduction of equal pay for women.

BUSINESS AND NATURE

The influence of the value of nature upon business has already been immense. At one extreme, vast wealth and enormous industrial resources were devoted to putting man on the moon by 1970, as President Kennedy in 1960 had committed America to do. Never had the value of nature received such a votive offering. Although the Americans and all humanity believed that they had stormed the proud gateway to the universe, in truth nature personified by that remote, beautiful and barren moon, had further conquered man. At the other extreme, in daily life, a national British airline in 1970 paid its tribute to ecology by dropping turtle soup from its menu, on the grounds that the turtle is declining too rapidly in numbers.

Yet tactical withdrawals on such matters as skinning rare animals, making nasty effluence from factory chimneys or dumping industrial waste into river or sea, disguise a general stability of the line where the needs of society can be urged *against* the ascendant and weaker value of nature travelling on its back. Thus we tolerate factory-farming, even though the idea of it increasingly offends our sensibility and the practice is denounced energetically enough on moral grounds by a small minority, simply because our large urban society needs an abundant supply of cheap food.

The move for an essentially defensive stance, which views the preservation of the environment and the conservation of natural resources merely as a limitation on profit-making, to a more moral attitude which recognises the positive value of nature, is bound to be slow. Yet it is within the context of this long-term change of value that we can best understand the contemporary concern with pollution. As Lord Ashby, chairman of the Royal Commission on Environmental Pollution, pointed out to some 200 senior business-men in June 1972:

> Pollution is, in my view, a temporary malfunctioning of the present economic system, curable at a cost affluent countries can afford. . . . Industry will make a great mistake if it concentrates on pollution control and neglects the stirring of a change of values in society. We shall not, I believe, survive another generation without fundamental changes in our social institutions, among them the values which guide business and industry in supplying the needs of man. I hope the initiative for some of these fundamental changes comes from industry itself.

The effect of man on the environment, Lord Ashby continued is compounded of three ingredients: population, the goods and services people consume *per capita*, and the impact on the environment of each unit of these goods and services. All these elements are highly controversial, owing to their damage to well-established values of profit, money, society and the individual.

The controversial issue of forcing by political means a limitation in population is matched by problems posed by the suggested reduction in individual consumption of goods and services, with its dark threats of unemployment and a panic retreat from the doctrines of free enterprise and economic growth. The implicit change in the value system of industry is too fundamental for this decade. To force a reduction in the impact of goods and services on the environment by obliging the producers to bear the 'social costs' of their production, although hardly popular, is the least controversial of the three variables in averting the danger to the world's environment. It has the additional merit that action can begin today.

Therefore the third ingredient in Lord Ashby's analysis is the easiest question in the moral examination paper posed to us by the value of nature—and it may become compulsory for more candidates who must sit that examination paper by virtue of being businessmen. 'While heroic world-schemes for reducing population and consumption are being talked about,' wrote Lord Ashby in *The Times* on 10 March 1972, 'a lot can be done—and is being done—to diminish the impact of technological societies on their environment. It is being done because governments are paying attention to what Blake called 'Minute Particulars'. Already Britain's air and water are cleaner than they have been for a century or more; already the amount of pollution per ton of product manufactured has, for some products, been cut to a tenth of what it was a decade or so ago. This may not save civilisation, but it buys time in which we can do some hard thinking.'

Two 'work in progress' stories—one British and one American—may serve both to illustrate the possibilities of pollution control and to highlight the value issues it poses:

1. Cleaning Father Thames

In a talk to the British Pharmaceutical Conference in 1972, Dr. David Train reported that the Thames Survey Committee, constituted in 1948, had taken 15 years to identify the measures necessary for dispersing the liquid wastes which industry and private citizens dumped into the river in the London basin. An expenditure of £35 million since 1948 had begun to cleanse the river to the state where the water in all seasons contained a little oxygen. Another £34 million would be spent in seeking a concentration of 10 per cent oxygen at all times and in all reaches.

To attain the minimum oxygen concentration of 35 per cent needed for full restoration of the river, however, would cost a great deal more. 'The community will need to recognise that this will have to be paid for collectively through increased rates, increased costs of electricity, paper, petroleum products, sugar and numerous other commodities which are prepared and manufactured on the banks of the Thames Estuary.'

2. *The Automobile*

A paper read at the 1971 British Institute of Management symposium by Thomas Reid, executive director in charge of civic and government affairs at the Ford Motor Company in Michigan, opened with a reminder that the United States had been compelled to face industry's involvement in the total question of its social responsibilities a little ahead of the rest of the world. Mr. Reid described the moves in America to control pollution by cars:

> New car controls, for example, on an average, reduce hydrocarbon emissions by more than 80 per cent from 1961 levels, and carbon dioxide by about 70 per cent. Our 1973 models will make a significant start toward controlling the third major auto-pollutant, oxides of nitrogen. We have been installing pollution-control equipment to reduce carbon monoxide and hydrocarbons on all of our new cars for the past several years; and that, combined with the annual scrappage of some 7 million older, pre-controlled cars, has already significantly improved the quality of our air. And by the middle of this decade—although we aren't sure yet just how to do it—we hope that every new car in the US will be virtually pollution-free. But to give you some idea of the goals we must try to achieve in this area, US government regulations, for example, say that by 1975, no one should be exposed to an environment that has a carbon monoxide count of 8.7 parts per million for more than eight hours, once a year.

Pollution control is still in its infancy. The state of our objective knowledge of ecology neither allows us to predict universal doom

nor to settle down into a comfortable and complacent lethargy.
Lord Ashby has summarised the position thus:

> You cannot predict doom any more than you can predict that it
> will not occur. . . . We do know that some wastes endanger biological
> cycles. We do not know what the danger levels are, for they are
> below the levels that kill. What we do know is that some of these
> poisons are accumulating in the environment, and although they
> may be doing nothing but a bit of local harm now we cannot predict,
> and therefore we cannot take the risk, that they will not rise to levels
> where irreversible damage may be done.

Doubtless we shall see the scope of pollution control widen as
knowledge increases and experience develops. The World Congress on the Environment summoned by the United Nations at
Stockholm in 1972 has underlined the importance of paying
attention on an international basis, for example with regard to the
high seas of the world.

> Roll on, thou deep and dark blue ocean—roll!
> Ten thousand fleets sweep over thee in vain;
> Man marks the earth with ruin—his control
> Stops with the shore.

Alas, these memorable words of Lord Byron are no longer true.
We can expect to see a steady spate of national and international
legislation designed to compel all businesses to follow the pioneer
examples of those companies who are already incorporating the
value of the environment into their boardroom decisions and daily
practices. For example, laws making compulsory the full disclosure
of information about the disposal of pollutants and the 'ecological
costs' (or pollution price tag) of products may become common-
place before the end of the decade. Moreover, there will be
pressures to take these additional social costs out of profits rather
than passing them on in higher prices to the consumer.

CONCLUSION

Pollution control is perhaps the most tangible result so far of the
heightened value of nature in our times. Such objectives as cleaning

up the air, water and land will keep us occupied for many years to come. We will also have to tackle the problems of population and consumption limits as the year AD 2000 draws nearer. But business can legitimately claim that these larger world issues fall outside its terms of reference however generously understood. None of us knows yet where our present response to the value of nature will take us in those longer-term areas of concern.

Having abandoned the ideas of early modern times that nature is a god, either a moral mother or a cruelly evil life-force, we have worked out way forwards to take advantage of the better current (if I may make a personal moral judgement) issuing from the Christian tradition. This strand stressed the affinity and relationship of man to his environment, so that the whole system must be seen as moving or being changed together, not any one part 'going it alone'. Studies of animal behaviour have vividly reminded us of our likeness (as well as our difference) to the other living creatures, while ecology reveals the essential unity of the whole living environment.

Yet we are made to act within that system as well as to contemplate it. Something akin to the Franciscan sense of compassion or sympathy stirs more powerfully within us. We feel, for example, that it is morally wrong to allow men to exterminate a species of animal in order to become personally rich. Put more positively, there is a dawning sense of moral responsibility for nature, a sense that we *ought* to protect, conserve and advance the natural creation which non-verbally appeals so eloquently to us through its needs. When ecology and economy are in focus, as two eyes are joined in sight, then management in industry may come to be seen as but one aspect of man's much wider management of the natural environment.

CHAPTER 5

Social Capitalism

'If we could first know where we are and whither we are tending,' Abraham Lincoln once said, 'we could better judge what to do and how to do it.' In this chapter I shall attempt a summary of 'where we are and whither we are tending' in light of the value evolutions narrated in the preceding pages. In later chapters I shall move on to describe and evaluate some of the key practical suggestions put forward for raising the moral and social standards of business today and tomorrow. Therefore, in a sense, this integrating chapter is the hinge of the whole book.

As far as I know social capitalism is a phrase of my own making. It has been coined to define a whole which is more than the sum of its parts. The 'whole' in question is our total socio-economic system. The constituent 'parts' are the values separately described in the first four chapters. Each of these—money, society, the individual and nature—have claimed or been accorded a religious status as the supreme end of life and therefore the dominant motive for work. Disinfected from the aura of divinity, each has 'floated' as a value against the other values in the civilisation. Disagreements abound on the relative placings of the values, both in general and in particular situations. There is a growing concensus, however, that all of them ought to be taken into account in managerial decision-making. And the grounds for this 'ought' conviction are now both moral and practical, in an inseparable mixture.

It is not easy to define social capitalism more closely, for it has already defined and shaped me and you the reader. The best definition of social capitalism is the story of our civilisation. But one hallmark of social capitalism is the growth towards an equal status of social values (including for the present the individual and the natural environment) with the strictly financial values of profits or riches. Attempts to produce an integrating purpose for industry to span the still-existing gap are symptoms of this development. To 'create wealth' for example, is more in accord with social capitalism than to 'accumulate profits'. The former can imply a social reference; the other is a relic of the old-style capitalism.

Social capitalism is certainly more than a matter of words: it represents an important and continuing shift in the value system of our common life. Strictly speaking, there are no new values, for values are timeless. But our valuing faculties are now more sensitive to a whole range of values impinging upon industrial working life. The relation of language to values is really a separate topic. Some businessmen and trade union leaders who have spoken or written eloquently in praise of 'social responsibility' are cynically insincere, in private avidly pursuing maximum profit on capital or labour; other genuine men, burdened by inadequate philosophies or ideologies, both are and do good far beyond the expectations of their single-value beliefs. To reach a true estimate of any person or company we have to look and listen continually to what actually happens, not primarily to what is said or written.

On the other hand, the spoken or written word can be both the expression of what is happening now and also an instrument guiding social change for the future. As words have a life of their own, establishing a kind of independence from their author, the motives or intentions of the latter, or his own degree of moral behaviour, cease to be the main considerations. Sometimes a writer or political orator may only be mouthing the inarticulate spirit of the times, himself unaffected or moved, like a chemical catalyst in a bubbling potion. If truth or goodness may be read into his words, they may bring results the author would heartily dislike. Consequently the sheer spate of words in praise of social capitalism, whatever the motivation of the speakers, builds bricks upon the foundation walls I have described in the earlier chapters. It would be foolish to measure real progress by these voluble professions of good will.

One characteristic early form of expressing the emerging value system of social capitalism, still fairly common, simply listed the human interests which had to be now taken into account in decision-making: shareholders, customers, employees, consumers and even competitors. A second generation of form is distinguished by a stress upon the company as a microcosm of society, with a necessity to conform to its minimum legal standards for good conduct and with a certain freedom to be actually better than the social average. For example, Henry Ford II in 1961 could declare:

> A corporation may be primarily a producer of goods, but it is more than just that; it is a small society within society, one with motivations, with rules and principles of its own. It is a purposeful organisation that can and must give more than just money to those who serve it, and those it serves. It should reflect in its daily actions the principles and aspirations of our society in its finest tradition.

Now and again, a particular issue or personality throws into high relief the trend towards a full realisation of social capitalism far more vividly than any book, article or speech. In 1973, for example, the case of the Distillers Company, compelled by social pressures to increase their offer of compensation to thalidomide children at the expense of profits, may one day rank in the history of social capitalism in much the same way as John Hampden's refusal to pay Ship Money in constitutional history. An outline story of the thalidomide compensation case comes in Chapter 9, but a felicitous statement it evoked of 'what is happening and whither we are tending' from the editor of *Management Today*, one of Britain's most influential business journals, is relevant here. In December 1972, while the storm over the thalidomide children raged in the press, he gave expression to a general feeling about the relation of management to morality:

Management need feel no shame about devoting its efforts to extracting the highest available return on its assets, so long as its actions and intentions are good—but good by whose standards? No doubt the Distillers Company, for example, feels absolutely certain that its behaviour over the thalidomide issue is beyond reproach.... But the management's conduct looks utterly different to outside eyes: and a company cannot afford (even in material terms) to appear indifferent, or concerned only with money or legalities, when permanently maimed children are involved.

The moral issue here may look especially clear, but nearly all of the concrete problems which crop up in the world of management and morality are equally transparent. There is only one side to questions such as whether workers should have decent working conditions, or whether firms should make the maximum efforts to secure alternative jobs for the redundant. Of course, they should: and those firms which fail these moral tests, irrespective of the short-term financial benefit, are laying up a store of serious material problems for the future. Nevertheless, the point of treating people decently—whether employees, customers or suppliers—is not because it pays to do so, but because there is no other defensible method of behaviour.

Seen in this light, the need is not for some moral rearmament of British boardrooms, or for the establishment of new, non-profit corporate objectives, or for the provision of a business moral lead to society. Business is society, and society embraces business. Common ethical notions apply to all society's institutions, and the corporations are in no sense immune from the restraints and obligations of whatever society at a given time holds to be good and proper. It is true, sadly, that businesses do sometimes behave in ways which in a private individual would be considered despicable, even criminal. But no answer to that misconduct can be found in *new* codes of morality: the answer lies in the age-old necessity of individuals to realise that they are human beings first and servants of institutions second.

PUBLIC PROFITS AND PRIVATE GAINS

Social capitalism is emergent rather than achieved. Each crest surmounted reveals a further ridge between us and the cloud-shrouded summit. Nowhere is this provisional incompleteness more evident than in our rapidly changing attitude to profit. For a significant period of one thousand years or more, it will be recollected, the fact of profit or gain stood condemned as an infringement of the natural moral law of equivalent dealing, which I have called the primitive ethic. Money first, and then profit, received partial emancipation from the thrall of religion and morality, but the dominance of the profit motive in a person has never quite escaped their clutches. Thus a certain moral ambivalence clings tenaciously to business. Under the protection of the new secular gods of society, the individual and nature, morality made a strong come-back into the allegedly amoral world of the market place jostling for maximum profits. The current belief in our present social capitalist society could be neatly summarised thus: 'There is nothing either moral or immoral in the profit itself: only in the methods by which the profit is made and in the uses to which the profit is put.'

But an obeisance to the social responsibility of business as the creator of wealth, supplier of goods and services and good employer of people, coupled with an adherence to codes of ethics listing bad methods of making money, does not close the moral question. There remains the unpalatable fact that profit in the sense of surplus value received over and above what is given in the cost of materials, wages and all other conceivable expenses, is an example of injustice. If the justice of equivalent dealing is accepted, gains in the real meaning of the word are immoral.

Hence the moral dilemma in social capitalism. Profits are needed to keep the system working, just as steam is necessary in a steam engine. Yet a sense of the immorality of profit still survives and even flourishes among us, despite every modern philosophical, theological and public relations effort to exterminate it. It is the failure to recognise this dilemma, as the *Management Today* editorial of December 1972 pointed out, that renders so much of the current writing on social capitalism both superficial and largely innocuous:

> ... Nothing achieves greater response from an audience of managers these days than an eloquent address on the ethical or moral responsibilities of management. In most managers, it seems, lurks a deep

uncertainty about ends and means, a fervent wish to be reassured that their activities can be justified in terms other than the purely economic. There is nothing wrong, and a great deal that is admirable, in both the uncertainty and in the need for reassurance. But business managers are nevertheless almost the only group in the country who see this apparently imponderable question of the ethical quality of their aims and activities as a major and engrossing problem.

The thesis of the business moralist has been beautifully set out by Graham Turner in his John Player Award paper, *Towards a New Philosophy for Industry and Society*. He argues that an increase in greed is a marked characteristic of our present-day society; that such untrammelled greed is a destructive force; and that industry and commerce, by working out a new ideology of unselfishness, can play a vital part in changing society for the better—indeed, in averting the potential destruction of society as we know it. 'Nothing would have a greater impact in changing the tenor of a materialistic society than capitalists acting beyond self-interest,' he writes. Britain's boardrooms need to be inhabited by people who are willing 'to subordinate material gain to moral values'—and this is a call which, unlikely though it may seem, appears to strike an immediate echo in the boardrooms themselves.

The stumbling block, as always, is profit. Turner's passage on this point is typical of a widespread school of thought. 'I am *not* against profit, prosperity or growth, far from it. Profit is a necessary measure of efficiency. It is not, however, an end in itself, and I am certainly against those who preach the maximisation of profits at the expense of a company's wider responsibilities.' The author here first issues a blanket disclaimer; then taps profit benignly as a kind of barometer (which it isn't); announces that it is certainly *not* something which it very often is (an end in itself); and finally opposes in downright fashion a preaching which has never been heard even from the most materialist lips of the present day. There may be capitalists who would grind the faces of the poor, or of their grandmothers, to squeeze out the last ounce of profit—but they certainly don't say so, and they have no apologists to do the saying for them.

It needs to be understood at the outset that all profit involves demanding and obtaining from somebody else a price which is greater than the cost of whatever product or service is being offered. If the supplier only breaks even, or makes a loss, he is creating no new resources, either for the business or for himself. Nor is he earning any return on the money invested—and the idea of profit also derives directly from the theory that a man deserves a rent for the use of his money. How great a profit margin should be therefore equates with the question of how high a money rent should go; and this is an unsettled argument which stretches all the way back to the Middle Ages, when disapproval of usury was as great as Karl Marx's hatred, in much later years, of the 'surplus value' created from the toil of the workers.

Under any economic system, however, capital can only be created out of surplus value. Under a system of private ownership, that surplus value is inevitably translated into private profit. It makes no moral difference whether the profit is the difference between the purchase and selling price of a man's own house, say, or the millions made . . . in building up Brentford Nylons.

One possible way of easing the moral dilemma at the heart of social capitalism may lie in the very distinction between private and corporate profit skated over in the closing paragraph of the editorial. In our society a 'moral difference' between profit as a function within the economic system and profit as private gain could well develop, and be reflected to a much greater degree than at present in the statutes and laws of social capitalist nations. Human nature and the doctrine of maximum individual freedom will ensure that the move towards a fairer distribution of wealth is extremely slow. But we may find ourselves acclimatised to accept only very small levels of personal profit, disguised by large gross figures before tax or duties.

Much will depend upon the eventual strength of the non-financial motives for work, still as yet trying out their wings. For one of the major fears in social capitalism stems from a confusion between the profit motive and virility or masculinity, an attitude which possibly has roots in our hunting past when we literally culled nature's profits or mined its hidden stores of useful and beautiful minerals. It has already been demonstrated by the management profession that 'mixed motives'—part-financial and part-altruistic—are as powerful and efficient as the single drive of the old owner-capitalist. The modern composite archer's bow actually shoots further than the English yew long-bow of old. But each man (and each company) has to prove that fact for himself in experience, before he approves the philosophy that lies behind it.

Others fear that social capitalism will turn out to be soft and flabby, disguising its diseased and inefficient companies under layers of public money. For all its failings, they argue, the un-fettered capitalist system could be relied upon to eliminate the unfit companies by take-over or unchecked bankruptcy. To prop up these 'lame ducks,' to use the emotive phrase of 1972, does no good in the long term. Society needs its profit-dominated capitalists just as a garden must have its scavengers. To freeze out the money-minded entrepreneur is to destroy the vitality of socio-economic system.

Clearly in the present stage of evolution in both social capitalism and human nature this argument has real force. There has to be a mechanism for change in the system, and profitability is one important yardstick of general social value. The unprofitable company becomes an obvious candidate for drastic reform or even corporate death. But the supposed option between softness and hardness betrays a false dichotomy: the true choice for society now is between softness-alternating-with-hardness and a flexible firmness. For the individual leader, in a like manner, the choice is not between softness or ruthlessness, but between laxity and that personal toughness which used to be called moral fibre.

JOHN BENTLEY: A CASE STUDY IN SOCIAL CAPITALISM

To illustrate some of these emerging patterns we might look at the career story of John Bentley, before he cashed shares in his Barclay Securities group of companies for about £1,600,000 in 1973. Possessed of much honesty, he has expressed openly his feelings as the social pressures of public opinion built up against his commercial activities. John Bentley's attitudes, as recorded, were essentially those of a capitalist entrepreneur of the old school, despite his comparative youth. But he swiftly sensed that the rapid changes in the climate of values had caught him temporarily in the open. Scorning the camouflage of hypocrisy, he has preferred

to re-draw and re-group his personal energies. Both his old attitudes and the painful process of learning were discussed in an
interview he gave to Hunter Davies of the *Sunday Times* some
months before the decision to quit:

> John Bentley is 32 and has built up a firm from scratch worth
> £25 million. It's a conglomerate called Barclay Securities. He
> created it in 1969 and it's risen by a series of dramatic take-overs,
> digesting the good bits of each and spitting out the bad. He moves so
> quickly that it's impossible to keep up to date with his deals but at
> the last count he was responsible for the lives of 7,000 workers. Last
> year he was the biggest toy maker in Europe, selling £12 million
> worth of toys a year. His pharmaceutical companies had sales of
> £20 million. He's now found himself in films, having bought British
> Lion for £5·5 million. It's like playing Monopoly for real.

> 'There's a general feeling that there's something wrong with
> people who get rich quick. I'm not an asset stripper, though outsiders
> call me that. I've only once had to make workers redundant, but the
> unions think I do it all the time. I've had threats on my life, Left-
> wing writers attack me, saying all mergers are evil. I'm afraid that's
> how the average person reacts to people like me.

> 'Unfortunately, it's now spreading to the Establishment. In a time
> of economic crises, pay restrictions, when the stock market itself is
> collapsing, they can't understand my success. When they themselves
> were successful they said nothing—that would have meant pointing
> a finger at themselves. But now they're joining in, saying 'if he's
> making money when I'm not, he's got to be wrong'. It's terribly
> upsetting.

> 'I don't like being branded as a wheeler dealer. We're just a young
> earnest bunch of guys, all sincerely trying to reorganise and re-
> utilise companies to the best of our ability, doing what the country
> needs to be done. I don't expect the general public to understand, but
> now it's got to the point where I go out to dinner and people point
> at me.

> 'I don't want to be known as a money pocketer. I feel I'm in the
> right, but I'm a realist and I realise that the mood of the country is
> against people like me. I have tried to explain what I've done, but it
> doesn't seem to help much. It's not just that being a capitalist is a
> dirty word today. Profit is a dirty word. Even *money* is a dirty word!
> I'm that big bastard Bentley, a millionaire at 32. I can't win.'

75

Social Capitalism

If he manages to sell off 40 of Shepperton Studios' 60 acres for property development, which was his intention last month, that could be another £5 million, all extra. It's a typical Bentley deal. He covers his outlay by selling off the bits he doesn't want, which means that he ends up with what he does want, all for nothing. It all sounds too simple.

'It *is* simple. I don't pretend it's clever. I've got a talent for making money, that's all. It's sheer common sense, as simple as turning off the electric light before you go to bed. Anybody could do it, if they wanted to know how.

'Every time I move I find the usual examples of British management gone to fat. There was one bankrupt firm where the managing director's chauffeur was living in a flat worth £40,000. Another chairman had just bought a second Rolls, so he could have one in the North and one in the South, yet the company he was responsible for was losing £80,000 a year. At Dorlands their companies had a total of about 25 directors pulling in £300,000 a year in salaries. That was equal to the company's annual profits. Yet between them they only owned 0·5 per cent of the shares.

'I make the very best use of a firm's reserves when I take it over. I promote young people. I put them through the mill in one of my various departments. When I arrive, the day of sinecures, of directors promoting nephews, is over. It's good news when I arrive. Shareholders are thrilled.'

But what about the workers?

'Whatever people say, the sackings I do are minute. It's only happened at Lines Brothers, and nobody will let me forget it. The firm was in the hands of the liquidators. I was *asked* to come in and help. We spent £1 million in six months trying to put the whole firm on its feet, but we couldn't do it. It wasn't fair to our shareholders. In the end I closed one plant, at Merton, and 1,000 men were made redundant. If I hadn't arrived, 3,000 would have been laid off. The ones that did have to go got double the redundancy pay they would have got from the liquidators.

'What I'm trying to do is to get a return, for every piece of plant, every pound spent, every person employed. The Government should be retraining people on a massive scale who have to be laid off. All firms should pay a levy to the Government to help retraining. I'd pay 10 per cent. of my profits, if other companies did the same.'

As an outsider, coming in cold, it is relatively easy for him to chop and change and, if necessary, close the odd factory. The City is still in awe about the speed at which he acts. But being unemotional must be his biggest asset.

'That's true. I don't know old Joe on the factory floor, or his moans and groans. Unions are always saying to me, can I guarantee the men's jobs? I say I can't guarantee my own job.

'What I do is I stand back and see the whole picture, working out the overall strategy. It's very like being a general, if that doesn't sound too arrogant. A general knows very well when he's sending men into battle that some will be killed. But he hopes that by losing a few hundred, he'll be saving the lives of thousands. If I went into the battlefield I'd be swayed by people. People would say, 'I've got a wife and kids, I don't want to lose my job.'

'But now I am being swayed. I'm terrified of buying any business which would involve one redundancy. It's got to be bad for the country. British business is full of bad management. How else can they be got rid of except by firms like ours?

'As a general rule, people lose energy after 40. There are exceptions. The highest paid man on my staff is 63 and earns £16,000 a year, but he's very energetic. The norm is for people to do their best, most creative, most energetic work before 40. Salaries should therefore go up sharply from the age of 20 to 25. It's the time when an executive *needs* a high wage, for kids' education, clothes, a large house, two cars.

'From the age of 35 to 45 salaries should reach a plateau. Over 45, they should start going down. This is people's natural life cycle, but people won't accept it. People will expect their salaries to go up, just because they've got older.

'It's such common sense, yet I'm called an impudent whipper-snapper when I say such things. It's a good job I don't take having a personal fortune very seriously. You should see some millionaires. I know some who'd rather lose their little finger than lose a million. I think they're twits'.

He's cared enough to devote his life so far to a job which has made him money. In many ways, how he's made it is less interesting than *why*. What made him bother in the first place?

'I didn't start off to be a millionaire. I was as amazed as anybody when I found I could do it. If you gave me £100 now I could double it by this evening. It's a knack I found I had.

'It was when I met real financiers and politicians that I began to gauge them and think, gosh, if that's where they are, I'm fairly all right. If they made it, why not me? I'm not senile. I'm fit and able to meet anyone on even terms. I was surprised for a long time that I could do it. Now I know I measure up. I'm not a fluke.

'The thing is, it's so exciting, building up a business, far more exciting than being a racing driver, or a footballer or a pop star. I have no routine. I start off each morning with not a clue about what I'm going to be faced with. From the very beginning, when I set up on my own at 23, I haven't bothered with routine things. I haven't a mind for them. That's why I always used to get the sack. I deal with the strategies. I have the right instinct for it.

'At one time men competed at archery or spear throwing or whatever, now the business world provides the arena. It's just another form of animal behaviour. You've got to be fighting fit to survive. I think it's healthy to be aggressive, to be able to match your wits at all levels. People say, here's John Bentley, he's worth £3 million, and they're impressed, but they shouldn't really be. It's just been a game, though with plenty of purpose. And the only excitement and satisfaction is doing it yourself'.

'I'm an example of free enterprise. I don't call myself a capitalist. I'm all for Communism in theory, but it doesn't work in practice. As for Socialism, that's the worst of all. It destroys the freedom of the individual, encouraging people to be resentful. Everybody is reduced to the lowest level not raised to the highest. Socialism is the sour grapes religion. It stultifies life. It's an inhuman creed. I'm all for helping the incapacitated, the elderly, the cripples, the weak in mind. But able-bodied people have got to look after themselves. I'd give them a bowl of soup, a roof over their heads, the two basic human needs. After that, they're on their own.

'People can't all be financiers, I know. They haven't got my attitude of mind. You can say I've done it all out of sheer greed and vanity. I would disagree. I honestly think I've done it out of an earnest desire to put my point of view, to encourage free enterprise.

'Nobody's shares are doing well. We're thought of as a high flyer so some people are looking for us to slow down. No, I'm not worried by the fall in the shares. It's only the personal dislike which upsets me. It's beginning to spoil all the fun. In the last three months the pleasure's begun to go. I don't know how politicians ever manage, being attacked and lampooned all the time.

'I've thought about politics but really, I'm as interested in doing something useful beyond politics. I know it sounds arrogant, but something socially useful.

'I'm still as ambitious and aggressive as ever, but I need some new goals. Most people have their little goals in life, a washing machine, holidays in Majorca. They're quite content to plod on and reach them. I've reached my goals so quickly that I've now got to create new ones. Making money has not been the end, but a means to lots of ends. I want to do something with it. I might help the peace movement, or spastics, I don't know. Making money is fun but it's pointless if you don't use the power it brings.

'I think it was Keynes who said that we'd look back to this present age and be amazed that materialism was our God. It's already happening now. People kill themselves in the rat race to get to the top, then they find they're not worshipped, or even respected, when they get there.

'I'm only 32. I don't know why anybody should be interested in someone of that age. I'd prefer to be written about when I'm 64. This has been chapter one of my life. I don't know what chapter two will bring. All I know is I'm tired of being attacked by people who don't like facts. I'm fed up not being liked'.

In 1973 John Bentley departed from the limelight, reportedly declaring 'I feel I have been consistent in my policies and actions. But I have been misunderstood and misrepresented.' His unpopularity did not stem entirely from these causes: it arose as the power of public opinion worked positively in favour of the value system of social capitalism in two ways. First, the spectacle of a young man out to make a fortune for himself may have collided with the emerging moral distinction between public profit and personal gain. Once more in history a certain rich young man 'went sorrowfully away'. Secondly, the prospect of redundancies offended a cardinal tenet of social capitalism, namely that the value of the individual (in the shape of employment) cannot appear to be sacrificed wantonly on the altar of private profit.

THE VALUES SYSTEM OF SOCIAL CAPITALISM

A constituent of our individuality as persons is our distinctive value pattern. Had we the means to chart the valuing activity of the mind in detail we should find that everyone has a structure of values as characteristic as his fingerprints. While retaining a basic consistency, these patterns may change as we grow older: within the value of music, for example, a person might come to appreciate Mozart more than the out-pourings of lesser composers. But to belong to a society or civilisation suggests that certain values are held in common. Put more strongly, society may have its own value system: there is within it a wide concensus of opinion on the existence of these values and their broad relations with each other. There may or may not be a coherence between the value patterns of the individual and the society.

What is the general framework of values within social capitalism? So far I have listed and described the major planets in the constellation, those who make their influences felt in managerial decisions. They will be familiar to any practising manager or company director who pauses to reflect. My job now is to see whether or not there is any discernible relation between them: to find out, in other words, whether values operate as a system or as individual meteors.

As my basic assumption I shall take it for granted that my other writings have established the probability of a relation between the three areas of *needs* present in any working organisation: the needs of the task, group and individual. Task needs cluster around a central human desire to complete or finish a job once started. Group needs signify the centrifugal feelings and pressures making for social unity or group maintenance. Individual needs are the range of physical, mental and spiritual needs each person carries about. In the working situation, what happens is that one of these areas of need triggers off reactions in the other two. A task abandoned, for example, may cause social disorder and individual frustration. Thus it is possible to construct a series of positive or negative interactions between the three areas, which I depicted in *Training for Leadership* (1968) as three over-lapping circles. They interlocked, but not entirely: signifying a state of tension (but not one of essential conflict) between the three aspects.

The three-circle trefoil described the interaction of *needs* in working organisations. What is the relation of values to needs? This question leads us to perhaps a fundamental issue in the whole discussion. In the dominant contemporary tradition exemplified by the work of Professor A. H. Maslow, values are the obverse side of needs. All that ministers to the self-actualisation need of the individual, for example, has value; all that does not is devoid of value.

It is possible, however, to argue in the opposite direction that values create needs. Because I see the worth or value of something I want it. The greater the range and intensity of my valuing the larger and more persistent my sense of need. Just to confuse matters still further, it is possible that I value some things because I need them, and want others because I value them. The relation between needs and values is a close one. From the practical point of view, there is no reason why we should not assume that values have a life of their own, as distinct from being the indicators of need-fulfilment. The *origins* of such irreducible values as goodness, truth and beauty remain a matter for philosophical speculation; the *experience* of values as powers not subservient to the needs of individuals or groups is at the heart of morality.

It would be mistaken either to stress values at the expense of needs, or needs at the cost of values. How far we sense the value infrastructure beneath the pattern of needs may depend more upon the strength of an individual's valuing faculty than on the 'objective' presence or absence of value. As one manager observed in an opinion survey on business ethics in management education: 'I try always to be honest with my conscience, but this is only a starting point; you have to develop your own conscience.'

Looking at values of social capitalism as refracted in a prism, we could do worse than beginning with the three areas which exert such powerful needs, sometimes in tension with each other and sometimes abnormally in outright conflict. The fact that most people at most of the time place some value on each of the circles often prevents a state of fundamental conflict from emerging.

1. *Task*
Task is a vague word, embracing purpose, aims and objectives

(goals or targets) in a wide sweep from the broad ends of human enterprise to the job you have to complete this week. Task implies an element of imposition, by superiors or the situation: it has a flavour of 'must' about it. A cousin word is duty, which conveys a sense of moral obligation to do a piece of work. That sense of obligation, as we now know, is largely a natural phenomenon: it is the 'lust to finish', in John Wesley's vivid phrase. There are traces of moral value, like grains of gold in a river bed, in completing any arduous task or challenging enterprise. But the natural sense of duty only takes on a moral character when the content of the task is good. The completion of extermination concentration camps for Jews satisfied the task needs of some managers in the Third Reich, but the value of the task was positively evil.

What is the task of industry and commerce in social capitalism? The answer to that question may be coloured by the self-interest (or individual needs) of the person who offers a reply. If our viewpoint is *outside* industry, we might stress the social and ecological functions of well-managed industry, and the meeting of human needs through fair-priced products and services. If our stance is *inside* industry, as a part of the system in some functional way—such as an institutional shareholder or an employee—we shall tend to emphasise the more tangible and immediate aspect of the task: to provide goods or services at a fair profit.

The two distinct values in this definition reside in goods-and-services (which are primarily good because they meet human needs) and in money. In a money economy these values cannot be separated for practical purposes. What constitutes a *fair* profit is open to dispute. But the word fair does have a moral meaning as a synonym for just. Certainly no one in social capitalism advocates that business should provide its goods or services at a loss.

2. *The Group*

As we have seen in Chapter 2, the working group possesses or acquires a value of its own. The more a person values this face-to-face small group the more he needs or wants to belong to it as an accepted member. The group's value stems ultimately from the fundamental goodness of all human society. As the author of Genesis wrote: 'It is not good for man to live alone.'

What is a small group? Definitions vary according to viewpoints. Wherever we draw the boundary line, however, there is always a distinction to be made between 'us' and the rest of 'them' in society. There is a value in the 'us', be the group a shop-floor team or the 40,000 members of a national group of companies. Within the context of a world society of 3,500 millions the most imposingly large corporation is still a 'small group'.

3. *The Individual*

The value of the individual as an end as well as a means requires no further comment. Even those who deny moral value to the task or group will admit that individual persons have moral claims and obligations, whatever their power or importance in the organisation. This value can be cashed into such large coins as the right to work, protection against unfair dismissal and job enrichment.

The three areas of value—task, group and individual—interact in much the same way as the infrastructure of needs. A morally good task, for example, enhances the value of the group, and adds to the dignity of individual work. An evil group vitiates a good cause and corrupts individuals.

4. *Society*

From the perspective of social capitalism the three-circle model of values is incomplete. It has to be bounded or limited by the circumference of society. Through the advent of tele-communications our sense of the value of national, continental and world society grows daily. The value of world society and even humanity, as a moral good, has a long history. The new feature of our times, however, is that a sense of society's moral value, which was formerly the possession of a few philosophers or saints, has become a passion for many people, especially the young, throughout the world.

5. *Nature*

The contemporary emphasis on pollution control is a practical and visible expression of another value: the worth of nature. We may have lost our desire to worship nature, or to project human morality or immorality upon its panorama of life, but its value has made itself felt in our corporate sensibility. Above all the 'needs' or 'sufferings' of nature have provoked a positive sense of its value mingling with our ecological self-interest in survival. As the eminent historian G. M. Trevelyan prophetically pointed out in 1931:

> Yet now that it is most consciously valued, it is being most rapidly destroyed upon this planet, and above all in this island. In old days it needed no conservation. Man was camped in the midst of it and could not get outside it, still less destroy it. Indeed, until the end of the eighteenth century the works of man only added to the beauty of nature. But science and machinery have now armed him with weapons that will be his own making or undoing, as he chooses to use them; at present he is destroying natural beauty apace in the ordinary course of business and economy. Therefore, unless he now will be at pains to make rules for the preservation of natural beauty, unless he consciously protects it at the partial expense of some of his other greedy activities, he will cut off his own spiritual supplies, and leave his descendants a helpless prey forever to the base materialism of mean and vulgar sights.

SOME INTERACTIONS

Both the outer circles of society and nature touch or pass close to task, group and individual. Thus the individual, for example, is not only a member of a group committed to a common task: he belongs to the wider society and possibly embodies some of its attitudes not to be found in the particular organisation where he works. He also lives in nature: at weekends he may fish the polluted rivers, or walk upon hills threatened by mining concessions and gaze down upon valleys disfigured by old industrial tips or dumps.

The task of the enterprise also impinges upon society in the guises of consumer, customer or its elected representatives—the government. As the value of society mounts, so does the role and responsibility of government widen and deepen. Moreover, the shareholders of a commercial company may feel themselves to be more members of society than of the firm. They are like one of the collars or clamps in a wrought-iron framework, holding the task and society together. It is possible that their role may become a crucial one in the future of social capitalism.

These values and their inter-relations can be expressed in a simple diagram. By understanding the values as standing or working in relation to each other, in an order or system, the practical manager may find it easier to know where he is in a problematic situation. Most soul-searching decisions in industry are caused by having to choose between values. The picture may help by holding up an ideal: the alpha (α) decision in the middle serves *all* the five dimensions of value which the manager embraces. Like all ideals the alpha decision may be rarely attained, but it is at the centre point of social capitalism.

The model may also be useful for diagnostic purposes. Sometimes trouble in one circle, for example, is caused by a value deficiency in one or more of the other areas. A meaningless task can generate individual dissatisfaction, all the more powerful in that the person may not himself be conscious of the cause. Too much value attached to any one circle produces another crop of problems, as the history of business in the last three decades amply illustrates.

Consequently the concepts of balance and compromise are central to social capitalism. Generally the manager has to seek a balance between values, however precarious it may be at times. In certain situations he will have to look for the best compromise. Codes of ethics, management courses, the policies and example of the company board all have a part to play in educating and informing his judgement. But he also acts in a system, as does the company itself. If he or the firm errs then the reality of social capitalism is such that there will be a corrective reaction. Thus social capitalism is essentially a value system, not an optional philosophy for some managers or companies. Of course within that mansion there are many rooms: some managers settle for the cellars, others for the higher floors. The majority of companies and individuals will tend

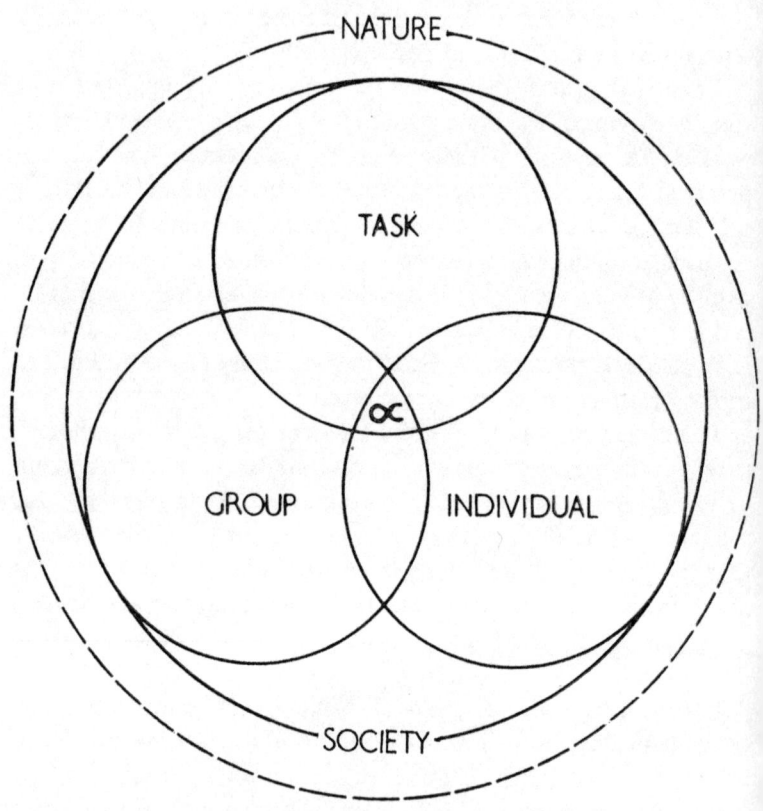

The Values of Social Capitalism

to choose the lighter and more comfortable rooms on the ground or first floors. As for moving higher, perhaps the best rule is 'All may, some should, none must.'

Social Capitalism

Social capitalism is as incomplete as a child. To some extent it is unfolding predictably, as if according to a genetic code of values which are the stored essences of human history in our present consciousness. Yet there remains a large area of freedom. There are choices to be made; each decision matters.

From the moral point of view, this liberty to make good our socio-economic system, or to debase it, has a value in its own right. For compulsory goodness ceases to be good. Although legislation in all industrial countries lays down what is in effect the minimum moral framework of social capitalism it is surely right that there should be plenty of sea-room, unmarked by buoys or navigation rules, where companies can work out their own policies and practices. Countries will differ as to how much self-regulation they preserve for business, both in theory and practice. But the risk of trusting industry and commerce to exercise self-discipline has proved fruitful, and cannot be abandoned if we would hold firm to our moral bearings. No freedom: no morality.

On the other hand, leaders in our developing social capitalist society will need a thorough appreciation of the planet-system of values by which they must conduct their free navigation. Consequently I make no apology for spending five chapters—half the space of this book—on those values of social capitalism which have claims on our love.

CHAPTER 6

Moral Problem-solving

People often regard making moral decisions as special kind of thinking, remote from other intellectual activities. But surely this is not so. In the first place we are rarely—perhaps never—confronted with a purely moral issue. Usually the ethical element is bound up with several other factors and issues of a more practical or concrete nature. It is true that we have a faculty traditionally called the 'conscience' which can pick out the radio-activity of good-and-evil, but there is no reason to suppose that the train of thought thereby set in motion differs in essentials from those we employ in the face of any decision or problem. Thus it will save time if we set the psychology of moral thinking in its true context, which is the mind at work.

A MODEL OF THINKING

In my book *Training for Decisions* (1971) I have suggested that when we direct our minds to work they habitually engage in three distinct but ever inter-merging activities: analysing, synthesising and valuing. Analysing consists essentially of dissecting or taking apart, and it is the mental discipline we most readily acquire through our schooling. Synthesising implies basically a putting together; it is the film of analysis played backwards. At the lower end of its scale we all synthesise when we relate two or more ideas or concepts together in our minds; at the upper end, beyond our imaginative ideas, stand those new creations of the exceptional geniuses in every field of human activitity or enterprise. Valuing is our inherent mental aptitude for assessing the worth of what is actually before us or present to the mind's eye.

Since 1971, as a result of developing a course known as 'The Creative Manager' in a variety of British companies, I have modified those basic functions to read: analysing-synthesising, imagining and valuing. In contemporary usage synthesising has a logical and artificial flavour; it can be linked to analysing as its reverse mental process. But imagining implies the ability to form images or pictures: it is the mind seeing things whole. Moreover, it leads more easily than synthesis into the central point that creative thinking is different in kind from its analytical cousin. And both are dissimilar from valuing. In reality, it must be emphasised, all three ingredients are usually mixed up in the response of the whole mind.

These fundamental keys in the music of human thinking do not only work on the level of conscious thought. The mind is like the sea, with its surface waters chopped and chafed by the wind, its translucent fathoms immediately below them and the deeper and darker depths almost beyond our knowing. I say 'almost' because there is a non-verbal and two-way traffic of communication through the various levels of our minds, by way of images, symbolic pictures and dreams. The deeper reaches of our consciousness, which may physically be associated with the inner part of the brain, are the workshop of the creative mind. Providing that its wiring is not unduly disturbed by neuroses or mental defectiveness the depth mind can and does undertake much of both the routine and the unspectacular work of analysing, imagining and valuing.

Emotion is not the same as valuing, nor is it the enemy of rational thought, as some have supposed. Emotions of all kinds and degrees of intensity accompany mental activity, and they may enhance and serve rather than disturb and distort it. Indeed some experimental studies on creative thinking have reported a 'hedonic response': a feeling of pleasure which arrives in advance of a discovery and convinces the thinker that he is on the right track, like a sudden sight of a seagull to a lone sailor on the high seas.

It would be a mistake to identify moral thinking with any one of these aspects. In any act which merits the name of moral judgement they are all involved. Analysing is necessary to distinguish accurately the moral question embedded in a tangle of other value components, themselves in a context of facts and a welter of experience. Synthesising comes into play when we relate the actual situation to some kind of general principle or rule. Valuing precedes, accompanies and tests our work. The middle reaches of the depth mind hold our tool-kit of ready-made rules and general ideas or values, as well as the bench upon which much of our work on a particular problem will be done. And morality, like poetry, includes 'emotion recollected in tranquility,' and also our anticipations of some emotion in the future.

Of course we do not simply bring these rough intellectual abilities or attributes to the work of thinking. They have been sharpened and shaped by professional training; they have also been fashioned by our parents, kinsfolk and by the education of our long school-years. That part of our depth minds we call our memory is stacked with both our own distilled experience and also honey from 'other men's flowers'. Our memories are libraries, lumber-rooms, cellars and armouries. Naturally what we have available for use in a moral crisis, and how much antique bric-a-brac we have to stumble over to reach it, is very much a function of the individual's life-story to date. Moreover, we shall differ about the status (or value) we attach to these contents of our mental armouries: for some they will be the cooled-down meteorites of eternal truth dropped from heaven, for others only subjective and personal policies possibly chosen at random. But most of us will have adopted a position somewhere between these two extreme points of view.

Lastly, we cannot think for long in a vacuum. There must be some stimulus from the environment, some context for our thought. Therefore it is always rather artificial to consider thinking apart from concrete situations. Our faculties are like plough-shares that need to be thrust into the soil of a field if they are to do their work. The average person's capacity for purely abstract thought is very limited.

THE PSYCHOLOGY OF MORAL DEVELOPMENT

The manager or leader in any organisation does not come to the seat of decisions with an empty mind. To understand our own mental equipment we need to be reminded of the stages of our own moral development in childhood and youth. From the turn of the century research into this topic has been conducted, but one study has dominated the field: *The Moral Judgement of the Child*, published in 1932 and written by the eminent Swiss educational psychologist Professor Jean Piaget. Based upon empirical investigations into the moral thinking of Swiss children between the ages of four and twelve, this work has become an educational classic.

Piaget began by exploring a child's understanding of the nature and function of rules in games. By choosing a game such as marbles he hoped to capture the spontaneous attitudes of the children, relatively uninfluenced by adults. He also made the assumption that the results might illuminate a child's evolving view of moral rules. While playing with the children he pretended to be in doubt about the rules and asked for explanations of them. He also posed such questions as 'Where do the rules come from ?', 'Who made them ?' and 'Can we change them ?'

The results revealed some differences between the younger and older children. For the five- to seven-year-old child rules were ancient and unchangeable: they were securely grounded in the authority of older children, adults and even God. Yet in his actual play the child was not above stretching the rules to his self-adventage. The ten- to twelve-year-old, however, thought that the rules had been framed by the children themselves, and therefore could be changed. But seeing the point of the rules as to make play possible without unfairness or quarrelling, he also accepted that they could only be changed by a common consent won through persuasion. 'The collective rule is at first something external to the individual and consequently sacred to him; then as he gradually makes it his own, it comes to that extent to be felt as a free product of mutual agreement and an autonomous conscient,' wrote Piaget in summary.

By presenting brief everyday incidents about lying or stealing and asking the children to rate the wrongness of the action and to say why they thought it was bad, Piaget also revealed differences in the moral judgements of the younger and older children. The younger could tell the difference between intentional deeds and accidents, but they placed little weight on the motive element. Quantity counted most with them. Thus one cup broken on purpose rated as 'less naughty' than a number of cups smashed by accident, or a harmless but fantastic and large lie is 'worse' than a damaging but tiny one. By the same yardstick lies told to adults were 'worse' than those told to fellow children. Lies were known to be bad because they are punished by adults. The older children took account of the material consequences, but put much more emphasis upon the intention behind the deed. So that, for example, a lie intended to cheat or deceive is 'obviously' worse than one uttered in ignorance of the facts.

Piaget then looked at the child's conceptions about punishment and justice. The younger child felt it right that transgressors should be made to pay for their misdeeds, and the form which the due suffering took was immaterial. If anything, the children favoured suffering meted out generously. They accepted it as just if adult authority ordained it. Moreover, obedience assumed for them a character as good in the moral sense. Lastly, the young child tended to see a natural calamity following upon a misdeed as its punishment, a concept we have already encountered in the Old Testament. Older brothers and sisters, however, saw punishment more as a teaching device to convince the miscreant of the fact of his moral offence and to deter him from further transgression. They believed in making the punishment balance the crime fairly. A child who takes food from his neighbour, for example, should go without that portion himself. The offender's circumstances and needs came more into the picture in establishing the punishment. Nor did adult authority loom so large for 'justice has no meaning except as something above authority'. For these older children punishing innocent people for the crimes of others (as when a class is punished as a whole for the offence of a boy who will not 'own up') is wrong. The idea of an 'immanent justice', linking fortune or luck events with moral behaviour, also recedes.

Piaget clearly preferred the older child's *morality of co-operation* or *reciprocity* to the younger child's thinking, which he called *moral realism*. With reciprocal social relationships there dawns the awareness that morality is more concerned with the social means to valued ends, rather than with obedience to authorities. Children may exhibit both these quite different psychological approaches in various mixes, as indeed may adults as well. Thus Piaget underlined the need to look for the dominating set of attitudes and beliefs, be it in child or adult. For the move away from egocentric thinking and parent-centredness towards operational thinking and life among equals proceeds with varying results in each individual's biography.

What the pioneer works by Piaget and others reveal is that a child's innate faculty for valuing in moral terms on the basis of what I have earlier called the primitive ethic matures with his intellectual and social development. Intelligence and social experience are therefore both necessary elements in moral judgement. But it should not be supposed that intelligence and social experience constitute goodness.

What the evidence suggests to me is that the values of goodness and evil are *latent* in a child during its egocentric and parent-centred infancy, and they begin to emerge long before a child is seven years old. Some children may manifest a 'good nature', a natural predisposition towards what adults would call goodness, while others exhibit the opposite tendency. Most of us straddle the middle of the continuum. In adolescence we become aware or conscious of the difference between good and evil. Indeed some biblical writers speak of 'the knowledge of good and evil' as the time when a child turns into an adult.

Until adolescence, as Piaget shows, the child articulates his moral views by a mixture of the natural but latent values of good and bad, the primitive ethic, and the first-hand or second-hand adult moral systems that surround him. In late adolescence, however, he begins the search for an integrating principle, ideal, or generalisation, which can harmonise these three presences. Perhaps the more intelligent and the more naturally disposed to goodness the boy or girl, the more important and intense will be this quest for meaning and purpose. Without waiting for such ideas his or her powerful impulse towards goodness will issue in acts of kindness and service. Yet the sudden awareness of irrational evil will at the same time strain the credibility of the primitive ethic as an intellectual theory of the universe, and may lead to the abandonment of the inherited religion or at least some of the second-hand adult moralities received in school or home. The chaos or futility of all things will weigh especially upon the intelligent and morally-aware teenager, and may linger long into manhood or womanhood. The results of this search—or lack of them—will be reflected in the individual's practical philosophy of life or code of conduct.

MORAL THINKING IN ADULTS

Adult moral thinking also perpetuates in a refined or sophisticated form the three focal points of childhood and adolescence: the situation, the primitive ethic and the values of good and evil. We differ, however, in the strides forward in our greater powers of analysing and synthesising, imagining and valuing, and also in the knowledge and experience present in our depth minds. For example, we are much better at analysing complex situations involving concrete factors and abstract notions such as intention or motive. The combination of social experience and knowledge of the vicarious experience of history brings greater focus and reality to the products of our imagining faculty: we can picture future states of affairs or consequences more ably. And the night sky of good and evil is illuminated by a dozen or so planets and a thousand stars of lesser values, which somehow have emerged into our consciousness and aid our decision-making.

We can therefore list some of the major factors which make up the moral judgement of a mature adult as follows:

> Awareness of good and evil
> Ability to analyse a situation objectively
> Knowledge of the relevant rules
> A trained valuing faculty
> Creative imagination

These functions, it should be stressed, overlap and run into each other. But if one is totally missing, then moral judgement is seriously impaired.

AWARENESS OF GOOD AND EVIL

As we all know, the vast majority of people become aware of the difference between good and evil long before they are physically adults. When situations are presented to us with the moral issue simplified into black and white, as in a standard Western film, we do not have much difficulty in sorting out which is the good side and which the bad. But in our non-fiction lives the moral dimension in a situation is often hidden or opaque. Moral awareness is the faculty which gives us an early warning, like a radar set, that some issue involving good and evil is present in the situation before us.

When this valuing faculty is turned in upon ourselves we call it conscience. Webster's Dictionary defines the latter as 'the sense or consciousness of the moral goodness or blameworthiness of one's own conduct, intentions or character together with a feeling of obligation to do right or be good.' There is an obvious link between the outward-looking ability to be aware of goodness or its absence, and the inward-looking work of the conscience. In extreme cases of psychopathic mental disturbance, for example, the inability to distinguish between good and evil externally is coupled with an apparently total lack of moral self-consciousness.

Moral Problem-solving

The faculty of moral awareness which enables us to pick up the faint and sometimes jammed signals from the moral clusters or values in a situation may become atrophied or dulled by neglect of misuse. There is some evidence that a person who acts frequently against his conscience thereby weakens its power to communicate with him, just as the oft-repeated action of killing—in war, for example—hardens its callouses on the heart so that the value of human life to the habitual killer is diminished. Action or inaction are ways of deepening—or erasing—values.

Sometimes the individual's moral awareness can be re-awakened when the more hidden and morally disturbing elements of the situation are brought out into the daylight. Memory may then remind a man that he had indeed received some obscure messages upon the radar screen of his moral sensibility, but—for public, professional or private reasons—had chosen at one or other levels of consciousness to ignore them. The writing on the wall of our mind is often so indistinct that it is possible to make out a case to oneself for doing so. Obviously the difference between this consenting self-deception and a pardonable ignorance can be marginal, and it is precisely this kind of hard case that our consciences must engage. Like the law, our consciences are not willing to accept ignorance as a sufficient excuse when it can be shown that we should have known better, or have found out before acting.

A classic instance of this retrospective judgement of conscience has been supplied by Albert von Speer, a top manager in Hitler's Germany. His book *Inside the Third Reich* (1970) contains an honest confession of his suppressed awareness of good and evil in relation to his master's policies for exterminating the Jews, and the later utter condemnation of his sins of omission by a restored conscience:

> It is true that as a favourite and later as one of Hitler's most influential ministers I was isolated. It is also true that the habit of thinking within the limits of my own field provided me, both as architect and as Armaments Minister, with many opportunities for evasion. It is true that I did not know what was really beginning on

96

November 9, 1938, and what ended in Auschwitz and Maidanek. But on the final analysis I myself determined the degree of my isolation, the extremity of my evasions, and the extent of my ignorance.

I therefore know today that my agonised self-examinations posed the question as wrongly as did the questioners whom I have met since my release. Whether I knew or did not know, or how much or how little I knew, is totally unimportant when I consider what horrors I ought to have known about and what conclusions would have been the natural ones to draw from the little I did know. Those who ask me are fundamentally expecting me to offer justifications. But I have none. No apologies are possible . . .

An American historian has said of me that I loved machines more than people. He is not wrong. I realise that the sight of suffering people influenced only my emotions, but not my conduct. On the plane of feelings only sentimentality emerged; in the realm of decisions, on the other hand, I continued to be ruled by the principles of utility. In the Nuremburg Trial the indictment against me was based on the use of prisoners in the armaments factories.

Gone for ever with these words is the belief that technologists or scientists could ever abdicate their moral responsibilities, or disclaim a concern with values. Rather conscience should be accepted for what it is, the radar system of a fundamentally good person. Like other signals its messages can be ignored, jammed or wilfully misinterpreted. But to allow conscience to atrophy through such abuse can lead to trouble, and its retrospective condemnations. Far better to see it as a moral awareness, designed to allow us to avoid the grievous agony of guilt. For conscience is a friendly poltergeist. As novelist George Macdonald noted about one of his fictional characters: 'She was sorely troubled with what is, by huge discourtesy, called a bad conscience—being in reality a conscience doing its duty so well that it makes the whole house uncomfortable.'

ABILITY TO ANALYSE A SITUATION OBJECTIVELY

What is a 'situation'? The word comes from the Latin *situs*, a site, and it means primarily the place, position or location of things, such as a town, in relation to their surroundings or each other. In this context, one of the definitions offered in Webster's Dictionary seems most relevant: 'a relative position or combination of circumstances at a given moment'. Webster also gives it the sense of 'a critical, trying or unusual state of affairs,' although this use clearly merges into the more common meaning of 'problem'.

There are several aspects to analysing a situation. For example, it is important to be able to distinguish its concrete and known surfaces from the more abstract and less knowable deeps of intention and purpose. To discern the ends and means, to separate facts from feelings, to divide motives from consequences: all these acts of intelligence come easier to the detached moral philosopher than to the person who is part and parcel of the situation in all its complexity.

For the emotionally-involved person his situation often seems entirely unique. In one sense he is perfectly correct, for all situations in life are unique—*that* particular conjunction of circumstances and people has never happened before and will not occur again. We have all had the melancholy experience of longing to re-enter a past situation, perhaps by going to a reunion or visiting some place where we once lived or worked, only to discover that—in the common phrase—'it is not the same'.

Yet the complementary truth also holds: no situations are completely without parallel. We can always put them into some general class, such as 'boy-meets-girl'. Novelists and playwrights assure us that the number of basic plots or situations they can imagine are limited. We seldom if ever enter one of these general situations (as I shall call them) which no human has ever experienced in the moral field. For morals are bound up with interpersonal and social relationships which have been with us since the dawn of civilisation. The work of analysis is not done until we have tried to place a particular situation into its appropriate class of general situations. Otherwise we can apply no principles or rules to it. Being a generalist in this way as well as a specialist comes hardest when we are being tempted to regard our own as a 'special case'.

Moral Problem-solving

The fact that most if not all our situations are less unusual than we think they are and fit more or less into a general category makes it possible for us to benefit from the experience of other people without paying the price of their mistakes. In particular we can trace how they have tried to respond to their values in that kind of situation. Moreover, these predecessors or contemporaries may offer us rules for deciding what to do in order to be good (or less bad) in a given general situation. Sometimes these rules may be grouped together into codes. Because they represent a bridging operation between values and unique situations they contain both value-laden assumptions and concrete elements mixed up as directions, guides or commands. It is obviously extremely helpful to know what are the ready-made recipes for action already at hand. We can identify five kinds of rules, which will almost certainly over-lap with each other: personal, group, social, legal and professional codes.

1. *Personal Codes*

From our family life and early education we evolve our own personal code of ethics, which may or may not be consciously formulated as a set of rules. Many of us at some time or other, usually in adolescence, have attempted to write down a Rule of Life by which we intend to guide and measure our conduct. In a civilisation so heavily influenced by Christianity many of these personal rules will reflect the teachings of the Old and New Testaments. Perhaps the reader will be able to identify at least one moral rule which he always follows, such as 'Always speak the truth'. Sometimes the code may be summed up in a more general principle, such as the 'Golden Rule,' or the dictum 'Do as you like, as long as you do not hurt anyone'.

We modify this personal code as our experience of life's situations accumulates. The research surveys into businessmen's ethics reported in the next chapter illustrate the importance which many managers attach to acting consistently with their developing but firm set of personal guidelines for good ethical practice. In both American and British studies, the manager's own personal code of ethics received the largest vote as 'the factor which influences you most when making decisions about matters of principle'. But the difficulties of applying the same moral rules at work as in the home or among one's friends received frequent mention.

In other words, an individual's code of ethics often define what he believes to be moral conduct in *personal* relationships. But much of life involves *impersonal* relationships, such as commercial dealings with people you may never see, and the principles of goodness seem less relevant. Hence the great divide which can open between behaviour at home or with friends and attitudes at work. The integrity of the individual, however, resists this division and seeks a coherence between personal and impersonal moralities.

2. *Group Codes*

Groups that remain together for any length of time develop their own 'group personality' and code of morality. The latter is enforced by various degrees of social approval or pressure, culminating in ostracism for the extreme deviants. Consequently the individual faced with a moral problem may well find one possible answer in the unwritten code of ethics of a group to which he belongs.

A group's influence on the moral standards of an individual member may be for the better or for the worse. One American study in 1969 found that the group's influence either way could still be discerned 100 days after the experiment, and that the person whose standards had been raised by his fellows retained his new approach much longer than the one who had adapted himself to a lower common level.

Group codes are vitally important where any common action must be taken. For it is the values and ethical practices of the group and not an individual which will inform the consensus or majority decisions. Just as the individual leader or member can influence a group's morality, so also he is influenced by it—for better or worse.

3. *Social Codes*

Looking beyond the individual and the group, we may discern another range of ethical guidelines in the unwritten social attitudes and norms of the day: the social code. We can distinguish this from the formal legal code—which at least reflects a society's moral assumptions—by emphasising its unwritten form, being more in the nature of those norms in groups which are identified by social psychologists. In contrast to the legal code these standards have no other authoritative backing than the pressure or force of public opinion, and its ultimate sanction again is social hostility leading to ostracism, that silent prison without bars or warders.

This social code of morality, often derived from religion, shares in common with an individual's own code for behaviour two handicaps. First, it is difficult to apply in complex professional situations. Secondly, the rate of technological and social change has speeded up to such an extent that they often appear to be out-dated. In 1927, for example, a writer in the *Harvard Business Review* could oppose some of the pious platitudes of his day by roundly declaring: 'The Golden Rule meant much in the simple, pastoral society with reference to which it was framed. Its application to our complicated industrial civilisation often presents an intellectual problem of great magnitude not solved by re-enacting it into a code . . .'

This point is emphasised by Francis Sutton and others, in a book entitled *The American Business Creed* (1956): 'The place of religion in the business creed is an honored, but ill-defined one. The creed bows to the importance of religion, admits seeking religious guidance, but continues to be a predominantly secular ideology.' The authors explain this gap or lack of influence of a majority social creed upon the business code partly by problems of semantics and communications, and partly by the underlying value tensions already discussed by me in earlier chapters: 'It is also related to a continuing inability to reconcile some of the teachings of revealed religion with certain aspects of American culture. How, for example, can the Sermon on the Mount be adequately

101

reconciled with the competitive, acquisitive spirit that epitomises our capitalistic economy? And the Gospel's insistence on the dangers of riches clash with the prevalent American attitude that wealth is a value in itself.'

4. *Legal Codes*

One solution is to make the society's morality applicable to general situations by enacting it into a carefully devised legal code. Law is the body of rules, whether formally enacted or customary, which a state or community recognises as binding on its members or subjects. This definition obviously embraces some of the unwritten rules mentioned above in the preceding section, but here I am using law in its narrower, technical sense to mean the Statute and Common Law. In the Old Icelandic tongue the root of our modern word 'law' meant 'something laid or fixed', and that suggests the relation between enacted and unwritten rules. Society at one of its levels (local, regional, national or international) fixes an accepted standard into a formal rule with laid down penalties for infringement.

The law is not morally neutral, for justice itself is a moral value. Moreover, the law recognises the morality which emerges in a society from instinctive preference and free debate. But our contemporary instinct is to resist using the law as a means for imposing the morality of a minority, however inspired they may be, by force upon the unconsenting majority. Lord Devlin expressed this view in 1972 to the International Commission of Jurists: 'The law must follow changes in morals and customs but in the rear of developments. Its function is to occupy new ground only when it is consolidated. It is for the legislature to decide when the time has come to consolidate new ideas into the consensus and likewise to expel the old.'

Therefore an individual hesitating about the morality of a proposed action may well find some moral guidance in the law of the land. Like many statements of ethical minimums, the legal code and the lawyers will probably tell him what he may *not* do, but then the knowledge of negatives—the 'thou-shalt-nots' of morality—may be a foundation for a more positive goodness.

The legal code, however, cannot cover every situation. Nor can we hold in our minds all its intricate detail. Moreover, there is a time-lag between the time when higher moral practices are hammered out at the centre points of social influence and the time when they are sufficiently acceptable to be made into the law of the land, especially when pressures on the programme of the law-making machinery are intense.

5. *Professional Codes*

Professional codes have some affinities with personal, group, social and legal codes, yet they retain a character of their own. Those occupying professional roles find themselves in general situations where the rules and principles of social or personal codes do not offer enough clear guidance. To cope with these uncertainties the professions concerned have evolved their own codes of good conduct. Broadly speaking, these define the moral behaviour which is expected of its individual members by the profession as a whole, bearing in mind its standing (or status) in society and the need to maintain sufficient public trust for the particular work to be done effectively. Therefore a professional code of ethics characteristically has both practical and moral ends in mind. It contains the profession's wisdom on how the inherent tensions between values which arise in its recurring general situations may be best resolved.

A 'role' is a theatrical term much used by social scientists. According to the social scientists, people occupy a variety of roles in life, such as father or mother, friend or neighbour, manager or doctor. Some of these are obviously wide-spread and some limited to a chosen or self-elected few. When an individual enters these roles, putting on the policeman's uniform or the doctor's white coat, he is also placing himself within the magnetic field of a particular set of expectations. These come from colleagues as well as the public, and they include certain standards or rules of moral conduct. It could be said that these ethical expectations are attached to the *role* rather than to the *individual* who happens to be performing in it. The professional code sets out to define the moral obligations of an individual in a given role within the context of the morally problematic situations which he will encounter in a working life.

The most ancient of these codes of professional ethics is the so-called Hippocratic Oath of the doctors. Our earliest surviving versions date from about AD 800 and seem to have been part of the contract agreements between master physicians and their apprentices, for the opening phrases bound the latter to treat the teacher like a parent and in due time to pass on to the master's children the 'Art' without fee. The ethical core of the Oath comes in the following sentences:

> The regimen I adopt shall be to the benefit of my patients according to my ability and judgement, and not to their hurt or for any wrong. I will give no deadly drug to any, though it be asked of me; nor will I counsel such, and especially I will not aid a woman to procure abortion. Whatsoever house I enter, there I will go for the benefit of the sick, refraining from all wrong doing or corruption, and especially from any act of seduction, of male or female, bond or free. Whatsoever things I see or hear concerning the life of men, in my attendance on the sick, or even apart therefrom, which ought not to be noised abroad, I will keep silence thereon, counting such things to be sacred secrets.

The ethical problems encountered today by those medical professionals who seriously seek to be loyal to these precepts illuminates the position in other occupations. The sheer speed of social and technological change throws up situations which are infinitely more complex than the code envisaged. The current practices concerning abortion are obvious examples of influences in society upon the practice of a profession.

Yet a professional code need not be necessarily immutable, nor does it have to become a substitute for the moral judgment of the individual. The advantage of a professional code lies in the stores of hindsight wisdom it should possess. For over long stretches of history the effects or consequences of certain kinds of conduct should be much clearer. As actors in an actual situation we may know some of the outcomes and guess at others, but there may be other latent consequences which appear later, to surprise us like the ghost at Macbeth's banquet. A good code of professional ethics should include these lessons from the past, while also acknowledging that new general situations emerge or old ones are so modified by circumstances that the rules can never be blindly applied.

A TRAINED VALUING FACULTY

The trained decision-maker needs a sensitive and alert valuing faculty, which can read a situation in terms of values and also decipher the timeless value systems locked up in the code or laws which have some claim on his attention. Moreover, he has to develop confidence in making judgements when two or more values are in competition with each. Codes of rules may help him at this point, or they may not.

Perhaps our favourite analogy for judgement is a man (or blindfolded woman) weighing two values in the scales of a balance. Justice means establishing an equilibrium between the two, but judgement in the more general sense implies determining where the weight of value lies. So that two courses of action, each with a different complexion of values, may be weighed in the mind—possibly over a long period of time—and the judgement given in favour of one alternative.

Some scientific balances can measure minute quantities. One luxury in moral judgement usually denied the practical man of affairs is scrupulosity. Our word 'scruple' comes from the Latin *scrupulus*, which means both a small sharp stone and tiny unit of weight. Thus a scruple may be the stone in your shoe: the uncomfortable feeling that inhibits action on moral grounds. A scrupulous man in this good sense is one who is careful to follow the dictates of conscience, and is strict in matters of right or wrong. In the context of moral judgement, however, a scrupulous man or woman may be too minutely exact or careful, giving an over-meticulous attention to the details of the fine grains of weight in the balance. This brand of scrupulosity leads to an inhibited kind of procrastination, and is plainly inappropriate for the man of affairs who must make decisions within time limits and in the context of a 'fallen world'.

CREATIVE IMAGINATION

Morality is not just applying sets of rules or juggling with values. Certainly awareness, knowledge and basic mental skills are involved, but they may not lead to an answer. 'A problem is only a solution in disguise,' it has been said. But the situation, forked over by the analysing, synthesising and valuing prongs of the mind, does not always yield its treasure. Imagination and creative thinking have to be held in reserve for such occasions.

To understand the possibilities for creative thinking it is important to grasp that good and evil are not simply contrasting values, they go together. Evil is a distortion or perversion of the good.

Goodness has only won when it has turned the acid acres of evil back into the farmlands of good. There is a transformation to be done, a creative work preceded by an act or vision of the imagination. We have to see the friend inside the foe, the saint inside the sinner.

Thus evil always poses a challenge to the good in humanity. Consequently morality cannot be just a matter of labelling names upon people, systems or deeds, nor of picking one's way delicately through a naughty world. To discover ways of 'making good' demands all our common powers of creative imagination, intelligence, communication and inventive ingenuity. Nor need they ever lack employment.

CONCLUSION

From this survey it is clear that solving moral problems requires a combination of general mental faculties and shaped intellectual skills, a clarity of vision, knowledge of the various codes or rules, much practical experience in a given field, a certain flair for smelling out where the right course of action lies, and a gift for original thinking. In addition, the creatively good person may be able to invent or improvise a solution, using the rules as a framework for fresh patterns of thought. We need such moral geniuses desperately, as a plague-ridden city needs doctors. For it is they who convince us that our life is worthwhile.

Such a variety of responses is rarely if ever found in one person. Therefore solving moral problems is better done in communication with others. This sharing does not necessarily mean an exact agreement on values, or imply a full consent in corporate decisions. It suggests, however, an attitude of openness to the advice or opinions of others, a willingness to listen and learn.

For individual or group, however, the quality of moral judgement does matter. In this short life, where so much pleasure and advantage lies at stake, we have to be sure that we are right to take them—or leave them, as the case may be. Only this sense of being right can sustain our wills, a theme I shall return to in the final chapter of this book. Nor should we place too much store on applied intelligence at the expense of a steady good will. For in the hour of crisis, as someone has said, 'Great souls have wills, feeble ones have only wishes.'

CHAPTER 7

Research into Business Ethics

Social capitalism in its milder forms found many advocates in America both before and during the First World War. Its most distinguishing mark was the prominent use of the word 'service' as a balance to the growing doubts about the traditional identification of private gain with public advantage. In October 1917, for example, the *Forbes* business magazine could declare:

> The square deal is coming into vogue all round. Rivals are treated less savagely; employees are not treated as so many pieces of machinery; the public are treated with greater consideration. . . . The business of modern service is service. . . . If business cannot be conducted under the existing economic order cleanly, honorably, ethically and humanely, then it ought to be swept away, and something different established in its stead. . . . Capital must adapt itself thoroughgoingly to the democratic ideas which have taken possession of the civilised world.

Such articles in *Forbes* magazine from 1917 to 1920 exemplified the general shift of opinion towards an emphasis upon the service aspect of business. But America, like all other industrialised countries, had not been without its pioneers on the frontier of business morality. Before 1900, for example, a character called Samuel Milton 'Golden Rule' Jones had not only introduced into his Ohio company the concept of a 'living wage', paid holidays and co-operative insurance schemes, but also promulgated the Golden Rule as the guiding ethical principle of the business. Recent surveys in the 1960s have shown how the American businessman's regard for the Golden Rule has not entirely disappeared.

The impetus given to social capitalism by the First World War contributed to its accelerated growth in America during the 1920s and 1930s. Doubtless the fear of socialism, especially Bolshevism, constituted no small part of this drive towards a reformed society: the American eagle must not succumb like its Imperial Russian cousin. Indeed fear of radical revolution, the force behind many reforms in Britain after the French Revolution, contributed mightily to the demand that capitalism should doff its iron mask and show a human face. Fear that the people, exercising power through lawful government, would dismantle the whole system of free enterprise and private profit, came hard on its heels compelling big business to kill the need for change by introducing its own reforms of the system.

As a feature of social capitalism managers also began to grope towards a professional status. For example, the British Institute of Management came into existence in 1922; the American Management Association a year later. The manager was not a capitalist in the entrepreneurial sense, for he risked none of his own money. Nor was he in the camp of labour. Thus management emerged as a 'middle force' between capital and employees, sharing many of the assumptions of the one and the status as wage-earner of the latter. Was management a profession? Some said that it could never be one, as professions existed to serve others and not to make money from them. Others, coveting the social status of the professional man, were prepared to consider accepting a business code of ethics as a badge of outward respectability, even as an acknowledgement of a limited moral obligation to the public. Still others thought of professionalism as the opposite to amateurism: implying higher standards of knowledge and competence, but not necessarily implying service or ethical conduct.

THE TWENTIES: THE RISING TIDE

There was much discussion about business ethics throughout the 1920s in America, mainly encouraged and promoted by trade associations. During that decade the majority of these associations produced a code of ethics for its members to acknowledge publicly. The much-publicised maxims that 'good ethics is good business' and 'he profits most who serves best' helped to reconcile the less morally-minded managers to this rising tide of social responsibility. Cynics like Sinclair Lewis might satirise such accompanying 'uplift' speeches and articles in his novels, but many clergymen, ministers and academics welcomed these homespun messages as evidence of a new moral and spiritual advance in American life.

In 1924 a Committee on Business Ethics, established by the United States Chamber of Commerce, produced a document entitled *Principles of Business Conduct*. It was a national code of ethics incorporating some of the leading ideas about the relationship of business and society. 'The foundation of business is confidence, which springs from integrity, fair dealing, efficient service, and mutual benefit,' declared its first principle. Such service was naturally rewarded by profit. The growth of social capitalism is succinctly revealed in Principle Thirteen: 'The primary obligation of those who direct and manage a corporation is to its stockholders. Notwithstanding this, they act in a responsible capacity, and in such a capacity owe obligations to others—employees, to the public which they serve, and even to their competitors. . . .' The *Principles of Business Conduct* also asserted that 'The corporate nature of business does not absolve from or alter the moral obligations of individuals.' Lastly, it hinted at one of the underlying pressures towards a voluntary modification of the profit motive, the fear of government regulation: 'Business should render restrictive legislation unnecessary through so conducting itself as to deserve and inspire public confidence.'

Within a year these fifteen principles had been ratified by more than 750 member organisations employing over 300,000 people. The President of the United States Chamber of Commerce in

1925 could thus confidently assert: 'Among businessmen generally there is a rising tide of conviction that business does not exist for itself alone, but is an institution that should serve the common lot and inspire men to give the best that is in them for the common good. This rising tide might properly be called the spiritual development in business.'

Some observers shared his belief that these early trade association codes of ethics were steps in a generally desirable direction, but still found them too vague, open to misinterpretation, and lacking the necessary legal status to make them really effective. Others saw them as gifts for the cynics: 'Compared with some notorious examples of business behaviour,' declared one observer, 'they are nuts for the scornful cynic.' More contemporary commentators interpreted them as part of a search for new restraints upon uninhibited selfishness, needed to replace the supposedly fading social codes of America's local communities.

The flavour of this new moral confidence of business philosophy marrying up with the older profit motive in the Twenties is captured in the pages of J. George Frederick's *The Great Game of Business: Its Rules, Its Fascinations, Its Services and Rewards*, published in New York and London in 1920—the year that America saw prohibition come into force, women's suffrage adopted, President Harding elected, and the din of European politics receding into the background across the Atlantic. Frederick, prominent in New York sales manager circles, nailed his colours to the masthead from the start:

I make no apologies for calling business 'a game'. I aim deliberately to encourage the idea of viewing business as a game in the best sense. We've got too good a sense of humor in America, and hatred of sham, to make believe that we're in business only 'to render service'. That's merely an abstract truism. Nobody lives merely 'to be good' or 'to render service'. Pure altruism is too thin a human motive.

Nor are we in business simply for profit—that's going clear to the other extreme. There's something else that drives the wheels of commerce, in addition to profit and service, and it is greater than either. It is the instinct to compete and use our faculties and see ourselves and have others see us doing our best in the arena; and to exercise the instincts of play and work.

This image of business as 'perhaps the greatest game left to man to play' enabled Frederick to write about the need for 'players' who know the 'rules of the game'. Indeed, 'There is no greater business need today than to grasp the rules of the game as they have now shaped themselves; and to play the same harder than ever before, *but with more sportsmanship*.' Frederick's evangelical zeal slowly took possession of his style:

> The rules of the Great Game are in process of being set by men of vision, by men of character, by law, by reform agitation, by Federal Trade Commission fiat, by self conscious action and resolution, by trade associations, Rotary Clubs, Advertising Clubs, Chambers of Commerce, and by the slow but definite action of experience crystallising into trade ideals and customs. It is time that these rules are codified and interpreted and studied. There is no more powerful moral force in operation among men than the judgement of their fellows in the daily work of the world. This makes business standards and codes the most powerful moral force in the world today, for the majority of men give greatest heed to the religion of the current standards of man inter-relationships, which are mainly business relationships and standards.
>
> Instead of permitting some species or other of religion to be brought *down* to business men, the business world has slowly but surely been bringing its standards *up* to higher levels. . . . Oh, not without prods, nor without murmurings from the laggards and tail-enders to be sure! Not without defections here and there, and stubborn elements who won't budge until the new generation takes the reins from their hands. But the push is on and cannot be stopped. The Great Game must be played harder now than ever before, to provide for a sick world; and the one lesson of the Great War is, play the game straight and constructively according to the rules!

Despite his highly-coloured and even florid pulpit manner Frederick retained his awareness of the distinction between wish and fact. Certainly he over-stated the changes that had occurred, but he had sensed the essential drift towards social capitalism:

As their [the captains of industry] knowledge of the great game has grown, and as they are learning to play it for the game's sake and for the healthy plaudits of a discriminating public, they are gradually losing their stress upon money profit and developing desire for the other kinds of profit that any great game affords. The game of business is in process of being democratised and neither money nor any one power is its autocrat. We have settled this, we believe, for a long time to come.

In his own 'New Business Ethical Code' Frederick concentrates attention upon the contact with the customer, and he naturally emphasised the practical importance of trust and goodwill. An ethical transaction must issue in real mutual benefit. Laws may protect the buyer, but the 'modern codes of ethics' are aimed against *indirect* misrepresentation, such as substituting goods other than the sample shown, or deliberate ambiguity in the wording of specifications. As an example of a step towards a 'business professional code so to speak', he quoted the code of the Rotary Clubs.

For good measure Frederick added a list of 61 'unfair business practices', focusing around the principle of *unfair competition*, which, he believed, had only become prevalent in America during the past fifteen or twenty years, as revealed by the work of the Federal Trade Commission of his day. From his study of its volumes Frederick highlighted such perennial industrial ills as industrial espionage, bribing the employee or agent of a customer, selling food unfit for human consumption, enticing away employees of competitors, and claiming or exercising a monopoly on the sale of products. As a means of suppressing, stifling and destroying free competition these practices were to be condemned. Theodore Roosevelt, spokesman of the frontiersman value of 'fair play', especially in his anti-trust legislation, had fought stubbornly to make the callous businessmen see the need to apply the same standards in business as they applied in their private life. The national consciousness of this need for fair play to shareholder, labour and the consumer, however, augured well for 'the development of the great game', Frederick concluded.

H

THE ERA OF THE SECOND WORLD WAR

In the early thirties the 'great game' had to be played in the drench-ing rain and cold fog of the Depression, and many of the players became somewhat dispirited. The general climate of disenchant-ment and defensiveness, coupled with the threat posed to business freedom by the New Deal programme of Franklin D. Roosevelt, altered the complexion of managerial thinking. Social and moral concerns, however, were not abandoned: they went underground, and received nourishment from hidden streams of individuals and small groups. In Britain, for example, it was the spectacle of the dole queues, the plight of slum-dwellers and the melancholy march of the unemployed which converted such men as Harold Mac-millan in the Conservative Party to the direction and tenor of social capitalism. The Depression was the Passchendaele of capitalism. Both officers and men, and war itself, were seared by it.

The turbulence of these Depression years, followed by the pre-occupations of the Second World War and its aftermath in the post-war period of reconstruction, did not favour the growth of business codes. Not until the 1950s did the social and human aspects of industry clamour for priority once more. During this decade, and still more in the 1960s, the influences of the social sciences, exemplified by such writers as Douglas McGregor and Frederick Herzberg, made themselves increasingly felt through management education and training.

But the social scientists in these two decades held no particular brief for moral values or business ethics, which some of them interpreted as ideological attempts at proving legitimate the illegitimate. Swayed by the desire to emulate the physical sciences they had eschewed such concepts as good or evil as beyond their field of study. Owing to the social structure of universities, which had led to the compartmentalising of 'subjects' into specialised boxes, they were ill-equipped by philosophers or historians to question their own particular set of assumptions. The orthodox behavioural science view dismissed notions of right and wrong as entirely subjective (thus inferior or unworthy of serious consideration) or else socially determined—the *mores* of a given group or society—and therefore essentially relative.

Behind these academic attitudes lay an intellectual agony, as unspeakable as death itself. It centred on the painful awareness that values had no intrinsic value; they were all shadows. At best they were existential choices of a courageous lunatic, determined to create meaning out of ultimate meaningless. A. H. Maslow, a patriarch of the new behavioural sciences, recognised this hidden malaise: 'The value-illnesses which result from valuelessness are called variously anhedonia, anomie, apathy, amorality, hopelessness, cynicism, etc., and can become somatic illnesses as well. Historically, we are in a value interregnum in which all externally given value systems have proven to be failures (political, economic, religious, etc.) e.g. nothing is worth dying for'. The formulation of business codes of ethics could hardly feature prominently in the programme of a decade which had lost its confidence about the very reality of good and evil.

THE RESEARCH WORK OF BAUMHART AND WEBLEY

In the first half of the 1960s Dr Raymond Baumhart, an American Jesuit priest at the Cambridge Centre for Social Studies in Massachusetts, set about discovering what businessmen thought about ethics in business. He asked them during three research projects in the early 1960s, publishing his findings first in the *Harvard Business Review*, and then in a book entitled *An Honest Profit: What Businessmen Say about Ethics in Business* (1968). Some 1,712 businessmen took part in his inquiry, 1,512 completing a questionnaire of 29 questions, and the rest giving information in interviews.

The Baumhart survey served as the model for a British study, which was undertaken in 1969/70 by Simon Webley, then Deputy Director of the Industrial Educational and Research Foundation. The Institute of Directors sent his questionnaire to 2,500 of its members on a random basis, and 763 (30.7 per cent) returned usable replies. After a computer had sorted out their answers, Simon Webley carried out 25 interviews to test reactions to the main results. In 1971 he extended the survey by sending the questionnaire to 1,000 subscribers to the journal *Business Administration*. As intended, the 442 who replied were largely in middle-management, the object being to compare their opinions with those of the more senior directors.

The limitations of the questionnaire method of research are now widely recognised, but it is perhaps wise to restate the more obvious of them. First, in all the surveys, 2,917 returned the questionnaire out of 8,500 who received it. One would dearly like to know what the other 5,583 businessmen thought. Secondly, Dr Baumhart admitted that his respondents (all subscribers to the *Harvard Business Review* or participants in Harvard Business School courses) were 'well above average in position, income, and formal education,' while Simon Webley was at pains to point out that his sample 'was ultimately self-selected'. Thirdly, it is not easy for even the best men to answer questions about their behaviour with complete honesty. There is a gap between our ideals and our practice, and it is natural to confuse what we should like to be or do with what we actually are or do. It is this outward standard of behaviour which others will tend to report, not seeing the inner world of a higher aspiration. Thus, without the evidence of others (superiors, co-ordinates, subordinates, friends and family) it is not possible to draw firm conclusions about the *behaviour* of businessmen from such questionnaires. Unless we adopt an entirely cynical view of human nature, however, they do provide us with a wealth of interesting and relevant information.

The overwhelming impression from both the American and British surveys is that businessmen on the whole do not experience a basic conflict between the demands of their managerial careers and their ethical principles or codes. One British director, for example, boldly stated:

> I think that my answer to all of the questions would be covered by my statement that I have never found that there is any necessity at all for there to be any conflict between Christian principles and business behaviour. I have never found that it is necessary to be dishonest or

that it pays to be dishonest in business. I have never found that the long-term interests of shareholders are in conflict with the interest of workers or society and I have never found it impossible to care for the interest of consumer and employee as well as for the interests of the company.

The statement 'sound ethics is good business in the long run' was accepted by 98 per cent in the American and first British surveys, and by 94.4 per cent in Webley's study of middle-management. In other words, the businessmen were virtually unanimous in perceiving a close relationship between 'good ethics' and 'good business'. During the interviews one in ten made some qualifying remarks to Baumhart on this statement, but basic agreement with it remained firm. Baumhart pointed out that the reasons that managers gave for coming to this belief varied, but experience received most mention in one guise or other.

In particular the businessmen referred to their experience of four results of ethical behaviour in the areas of customer or employee relationships: (i) repeat sales, (ii) better industrial relations and low labour turnover, (iiii) good reputation, and (iv) consistent behaviour. It would be wrong to conclude, however, that businessmen were only 'ethical' in order to make more money. It would be more correct to infer that they have observed in experience a significant correlation between sound ethics and good business.

It is quite possible that this factor of experience plays a major part in explaining the apparently more ethical outlook of older managers than younger ones as revealed in the surveys. A difference of response to the stereotype situation kind of questions led Baumhart to conclude that 'The older the businessman, the more ethical is his attitude.' On the other hand, it would be equally possible to draw the conclusion that, 'the older the businessman, the more likely he is to make moral generalisations.'

The case for Baumhart's view rests upon two points. First, that business success, satisfied ambition and financial security all reduce the sense of need for material and personal advantage which can drive a man into unethical behaviour. Secondly, experience has taught over the long-haul that good ethics is psychologically easier and legally less expensive.

Yet I do not think we can conclude that a younger manager is less ethical in his intentions. His situation in life is different from that of the older man. He is closer to the concrete situations in business life which throw up the more thorny ethical problems. He may have a sharper appreciation of their unique features. And his career prospects are often at stake. Moreover, he will tend to be less committed to ethical positions than his older colleagues, especially to those expressed in generalisations. These characteristics do not make him less ethical than the older manager, but ethical in a different way. Or, to put it in other words, he may have more moral awareness but less ethical superstructure than his older colleagues.

Yet these are differences only of degree. The overwhelming majority of all businessmen in the surveys did not experience a fundamental moral conflict as a result of their work. Most managers accept—at least in theory—some kind of limiting harness on the shoulders of their desire to make a profit. For example, 87.3 per cent of the British directors and 87.1 per cent of the middle-managers agreed that: 'For company executives to act in the interest of shareholders alone, and not also in the interest of employees and consumers, is unjust.' The American figures are consistent with this finding, 84 per cent of managers over 40 years and 80 per cent of those under that age agreeing with the statement. Thus the businessmen of the surveys did not serve 'the almighty dollar' at the expense of ethical considerations. They held the comfortable belief that due attention to these other interests would not subtract in the long-run from their commercial profits.

It needs to be said again that we cannot assume that the British and American surveys are fully representative. A more widely based series of surveys might reveal that this ultimately self-selected sample is typical of only a segment of managers in both countries. Moreover, one would dearly like some evidence from other parts of the world, notably Europe and Japan. Yet my own experience leads me to believe that the views conveyed by the percentages are representative of the mainstream of British management thought.

Whilst most businessmen do not experience any fundamental conflict between business ends and their personal standards, many do encounter what could be called lesser moral problems in daily life. The answers to two questions in the third section of Webley's questionnaire, as well as their equivalents in the Baumhart inquiry, supply ample evidence to support this conclusion. The 479 specific moral problems mentioned by British directors could be put into the following boxes:

Frequency of Business Relationship Mentioned Causing Concern

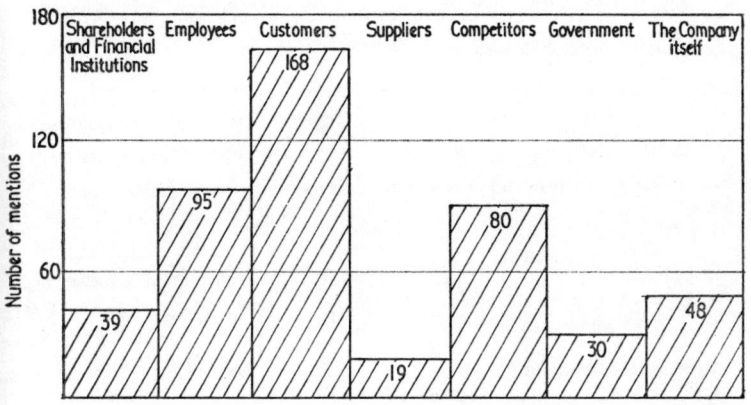

Diagrams by Simon Webley

Webley's own analysis and discussion of the cases or stories cited led him broadly to support Baumhart's important conclusion: 'The ethical dilemmas of deepest concern to businessmen are personnel problems; more frequent, however, are unfair competitive practices such as price discrimination or collusion, bribery, and dishonesty in advertising or contracts.'

119

When confronted with an ethical problem, what rules or standards does the businessman bring to bear upon it? The evidence suggests that managers resort to a range of codes for answers, clues or advice. The list includes the codes which have already influenced the manager's general thinking, and those which he might *like* to influence him if they were available. These are fundamentally the codes already discussed in general terms in Chapter 6, namely:

1. Personal codes of ethics
2. Group codes (i.e. the company as a whole, the boss or peer group)
3. Special codes (i.e. parents, teacher, clergyman)
4. Legal codes
5. Professional codes

For example, the British directors in Webley's survey answered a question on these codes as follows:

From your experience of business, how would you rank each of the factors listed below according to the extent it influences you* (your colleagues†) in making decisions when matters of principle are involved?

	First Person* Ranking		Third Person† Ranking	
	1st %	5th %	1st %	5th %
Formal Company Policy	17·0	11·7	27·5	13·2
Your own personal code of behaviour	53·3	1·1	35·8	3·6
The behaviour of your equals in the Company	0·3	58·4	0·5	59·6
The reputation of your Company	25·2	1·1	21·0	9·1
The behaviour of your superiors in the Company	0·8	18·6	13·0	8·6
Other answers	3·4	9·1	2·2	5·9

This list, it should be noted, did not include all the codes mentioned in my summary above. The middle-managers in

Webley's 1971 survey gave more weight to 'company policy' (23.1 per cent) at the expense of the personal code (49.3 per cent). In the American study some 807 businessmen answered the equivalent question, and they agreed in rating the personal code a clear first. Formal company policy and the behaviour of a man's superiors tied for second place, with the 'ethical climate of the industry' third and the behaviour of equals last.

This picture fits in with the general conclusions of Chapter 6 about the way the intelligent person goes about trying to solve any problem. Aware of the imperfections of the rules at his disposal, as far as their apparent relevance and concreteness are concerned, he may try out several of them, jumping from one 'frame of reference' to another in an untidy fashion. Or he may turn away from them and rely upon some sort of 'gut feeling' or moral instinct. In adopting these responses, it may be added, he is working in a world no different psychologically than he would be when trying to solve any other problem. The ingredients are the same: a *situation* with a problem in it, various sets of *rules* in differing stages of concreteness/fluidity, and the creative intelligence of the person concerned.

Both Dr Raymond Baumhart and Simon Webley go on to discuss measures for improving ethical standards in industry and commerce. The latter, for example, follows Baumhart in presenting evidence to show that businessmen would welcome the compilation of a professional code of ethics. Some 71.2 per cent of directors and 76.5 per cent of managers in the British surveys were in favour of such a code.

'Those who are most firmly in favour are among the under forty-fives, more often in small and medium-sized companies and those engaged in a profession as well as working in a company (consultants, for example). These figures, which are certainly impressive, are accompanied nevertheless by numerous more or less sceptical commentaries, such as "It happens in other professions, so why not here?" . . . "A code cannot do any harm, and should be beneficial in many cases" . . . "The code will only have a limited effect on the honest man, but will allow the black sheep to be identified and evicted".'

These less optimistic comments are reflected by the rating of a professional code on a scale of importance as an aid to raising the moral level of the company:

How do you rank each of the following according to its importance in helping to advance the ethical standards of a company?

	Directors per cent	Managers per cent
Higher ethical standards in society generally	30·8	28·3
A professional code of ethics of management practice	23·8	29·6
The inclusion of ethics as a subject in management training	18·7	18·6
A reduction in competitive pressures	8·2	8·6
Appointment to the Board of a non-executive director with a high public reputation	5·4	4·4
A social audit of the company	1·8	3·1
Worker-participation in management	1·5	3·9
An industrial chaplain	0·3	0·4
No response	9·5	3·1

The British survey also covered upon the question of how a professional code of ethics should be enforced. The majority of respondents (51.5 per cent of directors, 39.6 per cent of managers) favoured self-enforcement in each company, presumably by the board of directors. Next came groups nominated by industry and the community, gaining significantly more than professional management associations, with 'a government agency' bringing up the rear with 0.7 per cent from the directors and 4.3 per cent from the managers!

TOWARDS A PROFESSIONAL CODE OF ETHICS FOR MANAGERS

Since 1971 the endeavour to raise the standards of British business by the 'code of business ethics' method has taken two paths. A committee of the Confederation of British Industry, headed by Lord Watkinson (chairman of Cadbury-Schweppes Ltd) has looked into the possibility of devising a code for company directors, possibly with legal or quasi-legal status provided by the new Company legislation promised by the government.

Meanwhile a British Institute of Management committee has been attempting to construct a professional code of conduct for all managers. This particular enterprise is unlikely to succeed, at least not in this decade. For, as the director-general of the BIM, John Marsh, wrote in 1972: 'Management is a series of subjects capable of many extrapolations and mixes, and it is perhaps too much to imagine at this stage, that like doctors, lawyers and technologists, managers may soon find a common ethos, a common code of practice and a common social accountability. We have much to work for in Britain on this score, and must learn from other managers in other countries with their different styles, strengths and systems.'

This conclusion is strengthened when we consider the stresses and strains in maintaining and enforcing a common ethic in the medical profession today. If established professions have such difficulty in relating their values (in the form of rules) to situations thrown up by rapid technical and social change, how much more will it be within the field loosely known as management? Thus the tendency will be to produce documents which are more in the nature of philosophical manifestoes than concrete or specific rules. But such general summaries are unnecessary, for (as Baumhart and Webley help to confirm) the values of social capitalism are already firmly in the minds of the majority of directors and managers.

TRADE ASSOCIATIONS: THE RIGHT LEVEL

If the moral statements possible at the more abstract level of 'management' are unnecessary, where should we look for the professional codes which are, or should be, it must be stressed, a part of the moral man's armoury? My own answer is to build upon the green shoots of the 1920s and see the *trade associations* as the

natural centres for the formulation of codes of business ethics.
There are three main reasons:

1. *Practicality:* The function of a professional code is not to
   purvey values, nor to be a substitute for hard thinking in a
   unique situation. Rather it is to save us time by (i) encouraging us to place the particular into the framework of a general
   situation, and by (ii) providing us with a stock solution as the
   stimulus for our own original thinking. The general situation
   must be one which is practical in the senses of being tangible
   and easily imaginable; it must also be common to us (or at
   least possible). This condition may not pertain across a profession. For example, a psychiatrist may normally never face
   the situation of having to choose between the lives of mother
   or baby in childbirth. The more that a rule has the flavour of
   the tangible and common the more serviceable it will be to
   the practically-minded person when he needs it.

2. *Limited Generality:* Although a code of ethics enacted in a
   company would have the above characteristics, and also be
   more easily enforceable, it has one major disadvantage: the
   individual may have to be protected against the group. There
   should be some outside reference point to which an individual
   can appeal. A general body of managers and community
   leaders may well lack sufficient technical knowledge and
   background experience of the situation to make a judgement.
   Therefore, although wider than the company in question,
   the court of appeal should not be too general. Again it seems
   to me that the recognisable trade or industry in question
   would be the right body.

3. *Sanctions:* There is plenty of evidence that trade associations
   already discipline their members who offend against the
   codes of accepted practice. Two examples: an American
   journalist and her newspaper were expelled in 1971 from the
   Association of American Correspondents in London for
   allegedly 'violating professional ethics' for reporting an 'off

the record' conversation with Princess Anne; in 1972 nine firms were expelled from the National House Builders' Registration Council for failing to rectify faulty work reported by the Council's inspectors. Doubtless such sanctions could be strengthened, but in a germinal form they are already being exercised.

To illustrate the seriousness of a trade association's willingness to see its members disciplined the case of the fur trade is apt. In 1971 the International Fur Trade Association asked fur traders not to handle skins of the tiger, snow leopard, clouded leopard, La Plata otter and giant otter because these species face extinction. A three-year ban on leopard and cheetah skins was also recommended. Although the British trade in skins from the seven species could be estimated at about £500,000 annually, the British Fur Trade Association, with 420 members representing more than 90 per cent of the trade, regarded this voluntary scheme as an interim measure and was actually prepared to press for legislation in every country to prevent the import of the threatened species.

Self-discipline is greatly enhanced when members of an association freely debate and agree upon what are the unacceptable practices on moral grounds within their trade, itself of course subject to the overall value obligations of social capitalism as reflected in law and public opinion. For instance, a 1971 meeting of members in the 500-strong Association of British Investigators to consider a code of ethics rejected blackmail, bribery, telephone tapping, fake job interviews and trespass as means of getting information. They also disapproved of false negotiations to secure a company's manufacturing secrets, and hiring workers specifically for their knowledge of a rival's techniques. They decided that monitoring market surveys, financial reports and 'employee disclosures' were acceptable. Be that as it may, the fact that these detectives shared in the decisions enshrined in their code must raise their sense of responsibility for its observance, both by themselves and their sleuth colleagues.

These conclusions are supported by some American findings.

Research into Business Ethics

In a 1963 research study at the University of Tennessee, for example, James M. Davis reviewed codes of ethics in selected business associations from 1924 onwards, and concluded:

> A code of ethics should avoid the use of generalities, be derived empirically from the members of the association, and be enforced by committee action. If this procedure were pursued, the codes of ethics could prove useful guides to decision making and aid in the use of practical problem solving in the business situation.

Baumhart endorsed this view, emphasising that such sets of rules 'can only shed light on the businessman's decisions, not make them for him'. But they were useful for strengthening the weak, identifying wrong-doers, educating the young and keeping competition within reasonable limits. To fulfil these functions:

> A code must provide rules of thumb close to the real business situation, and as specific as common sense permits. But it must not be over-elaborated or descend to trifling details. Nor should it hope to offer a permanent solution to the ethical problems of business because the institutions and expectations of business change.

REFORM OF BRITISH TRADE ASSOCIATIONS

In November 1972 Lord Devlin's Commission on Industrial and Commercial Representation presented its conclusions to the business world. It advocated a Confederation of British Business to represent the 'indivisible' interests of industry, commerce and finance. Among the facts he uncovered is the startling number of trade associations and employers' organisations, and he recommended that they should be pruned down from their present total of 1,803 to between 100 and 200. Some 186 of them had incomes of less than £500 a year. Their distribution was as follows:

Number of trade associations and employers' organisations in each sector.

Agriculture, fishing, forestry	32
Mining	18
Food, drink, tobacco	128
Coal, petroleum products	8

Chemical and allied products	47
Metal manufacture	53
Mechanical engineering	96
Instrument engineering	13
Electrical engineering	52
Shipbuilding	34
Vehicles	13
Metal goods not elsewhere specified	79
Textiles	129
Leather, leather goods, fur	13
Clothing and footwear	45
Bricks, pottery, glass, cement	86
Timber, furniture	64
Printing, paper, publishing	40
Other manufacturing industries	22
Construction	393
Transport, communication	94
Distributive trades	269
Banking, finance, insurance	39
Professional and miscellaneous services	36
	1,803

Lord Devlin's Commission was concerned mainly with the issue of representation, and its proposals on that score have not met with enthusiastic acclaim from the main bodies concerned, such as the CBI and the Association of British Chambers of Commerce. But if its reforms touching the rationalisation of trade associations are carried through later in this decade we might well expect the resultant 100-200 well-financed and broadly-based trade associations to be in an especially strong position for framing, up-dating and sanctioning a code of business ethics thoroughly earthed in the realities of a particular line of work. The alternative in a socialist capitalist society is an ever greater degree of government intervention to protect the interests of the public, consumers, customers, employees and the environment, both at national and international levels.

CONCLUSION

Codes of business ethics have an important role to play, both in the system of social capitalism and in the moral judgement of each responsible person. To be effective they should smell of concrete situations, rather than the background values of life. An army officer, for example, wants to know the rules for interrogating prisoners, and whether or not it is ever morally permissible to shoot them, not to be fobbed off with a general principle about the value of human dignity or life. Above all he needs to know that there is a code of ethics in his profession, and he should find out what it contains and build its abiding prescriptions into his own personal code. So also managers will gain in vision and understanding if they have the chance to discuss—and perhaps modify—the present set of moral rules in their trade or branch of industry, commerce or finance.

CHAPTER 8

Ethics and Management Education

ETHICS IN AMERICAN BUSINESS SCHOOLS

The Confederate hero General Robert E. Lee, who became President of Washington College (later Washington and Lee University) after the American Civil War, is credited with the first suggestion for a collegiate school of business in the United States. The first to open its doors, however, in 1881 was the Wharton School of Finance and Economy at the University of Pennsylvania. Joseph Wharton, a Philadelphia merchant who endowed the school with 100,000 dollars and his own name, explicitly hoped that an emphasis would be placed in the syllabus upon 'the immorality and practical inexpediency of seeking to acquire wealth by winning it from another, rather than by earning it through some sort of service to one's fellow men'. Philosophy, history and the embryonic social sciences were to feature in the curriculum from the foundation year onwards, to make sure that this message was put across.

Yet the tensions between the university man's inclination to see business and management education in a social context on the one hand, and the strong expectations of the business customers for a directly relevant or utilitarian training on the other hand, made their presence felt in the pioneer decades. Although the 'broad view' of business education retained its advocates, especially among university presidents, the catalogues and programmes of the few graduate business schools in existence before the First World War reveal an emphasis on the more obviously useful disciplines and subjects. For example, the section of Harvard University's 1908-10 prospectus announcing the new Business School programme, declared: 'The School aims to give thorough and scientific intruction in the fundamental principles of business organisation and administration ... A broad foundation may thus be laid for intelligently directed activity in commerce or manufacturing, or in those specialised branches of modern industry which now particularly call for professional training, such as accounting and auditing, railroading, banking and insurance.'

From its inception the Harvard Graduate School of Business Administration strove to combine both technical and social aspects in the single concept of the manager as a professional person. Consequently it is possible to trace an almost unbroken succession of courses at Harvard from 1910 to the present which reflected a concern for the social dimension of service implicit in the ideal of a profession. As words are subject to fashion, however, the title of this series of courses changed over the decades: Business Policy, Social Factors in Business Enterprise, Business History, and Business Ethics—each had their allotted times of popularity.

After the Second World War all first-year students at the Harvard Business School took as an obligatory subject the linear descendant of the Business Ethics (as it had become to be known from 1931 onwards), then entitled 'Business Responsibility in American Society'. In 1955 the faculty introduced an elective course for second-year students in the same field. About ten per cent of them chose this course, which is presently called 'Business, Society and the Individual' and rests on the celebrated case study method of teaching.

A questionnaire study of the opinions of more than 1,600 graduates of the Wharton School in 1929 appears to have confirmed the value of courses focusing in an academic way upon the social significance and responsibilities of business. The correspondents then rated them third in value behind English and the 'description and analysis of business activities', but ahead of courses on administration. A survey of opinions held by deans and faculties of 33 collegiate business schools three years earlier had established that 233 staff members also thought that it was desirable to include a 'social point of view' in the preparation of students for a business career, as opposed to 15 negative and 29 doubtful replies.

Yet the extent and the acceptance of courses in business ethics and the social responsibility of industry in America should not be exaggerated. Apart from the cynics who merely dismissed these studies as 'moral uplift', there were plenty of enthusiastic advocates of the 'social point of view', such as Wallace B. Donham (Dean of the Harvard Business School in the 1920s), who showed an awareness of how little effect their courses were having on the actual practices of business. Moreover, as management education grew so rapidly in the period between 1930 and 1970 outside the universities, the advocates of a narrow interpretation of business professionalism tended to win the day. Eloquent speeches on the social nature of business still adorned the gatherings of business school graduates during this period, however, and the vision of the 'founding fathers' of American business education remained in the background.

The Baumhart survey (1968) raised questions about the value of courses on the wider moral and social responsibilities of management, courses which had so far survived the strong pressures to oust them altogether from the curriculum. Some 35 per cent of 514 managers in the survey had taken a course in college on ethics or moral philosophy, but they did not differ significantly in their replies to nine particular ethical questions from those who had not undergone such programmes. Yet Baumhart pointed out that the questions selected for the comparison had not been very complex or searching ones. Moreover, the courses concerned had been isolated from business, being composed of moral philosophy's theories and principles. There had been no specific or concrete cases to involve the student in the problems and discoveries of application. Yet Baumhart concluded that even such general courses might develop sensitivity to moral issues, a higher quality of thinking and reasoning, and a clearer expression of ideas.

Baumhart noted also the tendency to drop from course titles the word 'ethics' in favour of such phrases as 'social responsibility' or 'human challenge', quoting Professor Michael Fogarty's comment that 'Ethics, unlike the rose, smells sweeter by almost any other name.' Moreover, the word ethics has acquired some distinctive overtones. As Robert Bridges declared in *Testament of Beauty*: 'When men speak of ethics, 'tis of sex they think; for why the passion of it both transporteth their souls and troubleth daily life with problems of conduct.'

Baumhart also referred to a Harvard Business School study by Professor K. Andrews, entitled *The Effectiveness of University Development Programs* (1966), in which an encouraging 13 per cent of 6,000 managers on some 39 different courses (varying in length from two to sixteen weeks) spoke of the 'ethical impact' they had received. There were wide variations of response in this respect to particular programmes: no graduates who had been on two of the courses reported learning anything, while as many as 33 per cent at another centre referred to their positive discoveries in moral thinking. Why the difference? The programmes which were more often mentioned favourably had four characteristics:

1. Ethical issues were explicitly raised in the curriculum;
2. Opportunities existed for class discussion, usually through cases;
3. The teachers were vital and capable;
4. The programmes tended to be those of longer duration.

A survey by W. Ruder in 1962, sponsored by the Business Ethics Advisory Council of the Secretary of Commerce, confirmed the critical importance of the supply of suitable teachers. Several business schools did not offer a course 'as they lacked qualified teachers, while five others had dropped the subject because of diminished student interest. Seventy business school deans (out of the 104 approached) reported that they would like to tackle the subject of Business Ethics (alias Responsibilities of Business Leaders, alias Social Philosophy of Business, alias Business and Society, etc.) along the following lines:

Offer a course in *general* ethics and integrate ethics into business
  courses   7
Offer a course in *business* ethics and integrate ethics into business
  courses   14
Offer *no separate course*, but integrate ethics into business courses 49

Thus the majority favoured the method of teaching which placed business ethics into the context of the value system which will underline all the decisions made by a businessman. Baumhart, however, agreed with the dean who wrote: 'This subject should be approached on a formal course basis but, and this is very important, this course should be supplemented by discussion of ethical questions in all courses wherever these issues are relevant.' Yet Baumhart saw two difficulties: establishing the right place for the business ethics course in the curriculum, and providing exceptional teachers who would attract students to a subject which then lacked popularity. Also he raised the problems of evaluation for such courses, noting that 'There is no evidence that decision-making is more ethical as a result of college courses.' But he concluded that this fact should not be seen as an argument against *any* course, but more as a spur for developing really effective ones.

SOME BRITISH DEVELOPMENTS

For a cluster of reasons the development of management education in the United Kingdom lagged far behind its American cousin. Not until the 1960s did the British expansion really leap forward: both the London and Manchester Graduate Schools of Business opened their doors in this decade, and a galaxy of management centres at other universities, as well as such well-established stars as the Henley Administrative Staff College, added their lights to the scene. The larger companies and public corporations not only made use of these establishments but also set up their own training centres and in-company programmes.

During the 1950s British management education reflected the current American emphasis upon the professional knowledge and technical expertise of the business executive, for it was these attributes the British managers most admired in their American counterparts. Such areas as 'social responsibility' or 'business ethics' were dismissed as peculiar to the American culture. Thus British management thought centred upon obtaining the efficiency, status and social rewards of professionalism while discarding the value implications of the traditional professions. Although many older leading British industrialists spoke out consistently in favour of the development of social capitalism, their views carried little weight with the staffs of the business schools. For non-material values did not feature in the new orthodox philosophy of management education.

The development of British management education since 1967 has confirmed the trend towards the narrow definition of professionalism. But developments outside the mounting walls of business specialism began to exert their influence. By the late 1960s many practitioners of the sciences (including economists and political scientists) were beginning to accept and discuss openly the fact that their disciplines had failed to disinfect themselvse from the odour of values and by their very nature could not hope to do so. Professor Karl Popper had already pointed out that the physical sciences rested on a value judgement about the world. If the physicist could not escape value thinking, what chance had a behavioural scientist? It gradually became clearer that the real option lay not between some 'managerial ideology' and a purely empirical body of knowledge, but between one set of values and the value-laden ideologies of the various human or social sciences. This intellectual sea-change in the late 1960s and early 1970s could not be called widespread in terms of numbers, but it did begin to influence a British climate which had been indifferent and even hostile to the Harvard tradition of business ethics and social responsibility. Yet there remained not only the communication problem of persuading the rapidly hardening orthodoxies of the British business schools to grasp this point, but also the linked training problem of devising a method of teaching in the field of moral and social responsibility.

In 1968 these twin problems were first explored at a new conference centre, St George's House in Windsor Castle. Founded in 1966 by the Dean of Windsor, with the support of Her Majesty the Queen, the Knights of the Garter and the Chapter of St George's Chapel, as a place 'where men and women of responsibility and serious intent could discuss where their world was going and what they could do about it', St George's House had already seen a series of weekend consultations on business ethics and industrial relations. In December 1968, however, a group of heads of management education and training centres assembled at Windsor for the first of an annual series of weekends to discuss the place of ethics in management education.

Perhaps these British developments could be summarised by saying that there has been a slowly growing sense that values are vital ingredients in all decisions, and that a manager is ill-equipped to make critical decisions unless he has considered the place of values both in his own thinking and in the social *milieu* in which he must act.

Is it possible to train people to make good decisions? Certainly the nations adopting social capitalism expect nothing less from their management educators of today and tomorrow.

TRAINING FOR GOOD DECISIONS

Much ink has already been spilt over the issue of whether or not business ethics should be taught as a separate subject in the curriculum. The majority opinion has been against this direct approach, favouring the notion of allowing ethical discussion to arise naturally in the context of case-study work in the syllabus.

But there is little evidence that the study of case histories leads to the discovery of values or principles. Even if a plentiful supply of gifted teachers—with the brains of Aristotle and the experience of Henry Ford—could be guaranteed, this purely inductive approach would consume too much time for all but the two-year post-graduate business school programmes. Nor is there any sign that the compilers of case-studies have a range sufficient to capture fully the elusive and disguised value issues of a human situation in the medium of the written word.

A possible compromise between these alternatives is an integrated course on social responsibility (or some such term), which might include a certain amount on business ethics and some case-study work. As shown above, this solution has been the one traditionally adopted by the Harvard Business School. But it possesses two disadvantages. First, it can easily degenerate into a justification for big business, an ideological defence of the capitalist system, and such a 'soft sell' could soon lose the critical interest of a younger generation rightly sceptical of large-scale public relations exercises. Secondly, it includes too much knowledge *about* the subject and not enough emphasis on the student *doing* and discovering for himself.

My own proposed solution would be to introduce into management education or training a short integrated course on practical or applied thinking: an exploration of how the mind goes about its work of making decisions, solving problems and generating new ideas. This course would introduce the valuing faculty naturally as one of the three elements of thinking (analysing, imagining and valuing) in any situation. Thus a recognition of values would develop in the central workshop of management education, so to speak, and not in one of its outlying garden sheds. An exploration of values, guidelines and rules would flow from this consideration of decision-making and problem-solving. The actual shape of the course in a given business school or company programme, I would submit, can only be determined by a thorough review of the six factors I hold to be implicit in any communication exercise.

Ethics and Management Education

1. *Aims and Objectives*

Obviously the first principle in education (as in business) is to get one's aim right. Very broadly we could distinguish between three wide categories of aim in the educational and training field:

   (i) to develop awareness
  (ii) to develop understanding
 (iii) to develop skill.

These areas are inter-related and sometimes inseparable, but it is often necessary to establish the order of priority among them for a given communication. To do so it is important to understand their general characteristics. Awareness stands for the quality or state of being conscious of something or someone; it covers much the same ground as the more fashionable word 'sensitivity'.

Understanding here describes the illumination which comes from the interplay of theory and practice, or general ideas and principles on the one hand and experience on the other. It calls into operation our intellectual faculties, the power to recognise and comprehend meaning. The result of discerning and grasping the relation of the particular to the general is an inward change of mind which we call an increase in knowledge and understanding. In some way or other the mind has expanded its range, scope or depth. There may or may not be changes of behaviour in consequence.

Skill is practical knowledge. Normally we use the word training to describe the total process of developing a skill, and reserve education for the related realm of understanding knowledge, but the distinction is an arbitrary one. Flying a jet airliner, for example, requires both considerable understanding and a variety of skills. But skill-training is in principle much more measureable than education which primarily seeks to develop awareness, knowledge and understanding, for it is easier to test proficiency in a skill or in a cluster of skills which we call a craft.

The vast majority of us have the innate ability to distinguish the presence of good and evil, right and wrong, when they come to us in the extreme black or white forms. But we vary in our *awareness* of moral values when they are embedded in the concrete of complex situations. Therefore it could be argued that a part of the aim in moral education should be to develop the mind's valuing faculty, the radar beams by which we pick up the presence of values, as they hide in persons, policies or places. The first step, indeed, may be to persuade people that they do in fact have such a radar set in their minds, whether they like it or not.

Beyond the awareness of valuing and values (one's own, other people's, the company's) the development of *understanding* would entail the introduction of principles and rules. For it is knowledge of these semi-abstract, semi-concrete notions which enable us both to place our own and other people's experience into an appropriate context and also if necessary to act in an intelligent and human way. So understanding should lead to us the threshold of practical action.

The third general aim—to develop *skill*—would involve taking people over that threshold. The practice phase in which skills are improved might include 'on the job' situations as well as case-studies and exercises. The characteristic of this form of training, however, is the rigorous appraisal of how a particular skill is applied in a familiar or strange setting. In principle it should be possible to test or measure the skill improvement produced by the training.

In many areas it is possible to acquire a skill, with only a rudimentary wider understanding. But in many others, including the practical use of the intellect, it is necessary to activate all three —awareness, understanding and skill—together if real progress is to be achieved. Where course time is short it may be wise to limit the aim to the stirring of awareness. It is certainly a waste of that brief time to introduce skill-training in this field if awareness and understanding have been totally neglected.

2. *The Communicants*

In the past few years management educators and training managers have become much more aware of the existence of 'training needs' and much more adept at identifying them. Behind the evolution of this practice lies the obvious if often neglected assumption that training should be relevant to the present or future work of the person who undergoes it. Who are the communicants (or receivers) for training courses in decision-making? Why do they need such training?

Today, faced with the speed of social and technological change, the manager must not only make a continuous series of decisions and solve countless problems, but he has to develop powers of creative thinking and the resourcefulness latent in his own mind and those of everyone else in his team or enterprise.

To this general characteristic of our times we may add one other. People desire more and more to participate in those decisions which affect their welfare or work. Whereas an individual thinker can ignore the processes of his mind, being only interested in the results, this strategy produces only frustration in a group. It is necessary in a group or organisation to make explicit the phases of decision-making which lead from where one is to where one wants to be. Therefore the cost of the full involvement of people in the process of decision-making is the development of an appropriate awareness, understanding and skill in the leadership of industry.

Each individual encounters a personal kind of change whenever he or she enters upon a career, changes jobs or receives promotion. If we accept as a principle that if people are given a new job or responsibility they should also have the opportunity of preparing for it by some form of training, it is possible to argue that such further training should include (for managerial posts) an exploration of the nature and practice of decision-making, especially the full involvement of people in the process of thinking. And better decision-making must involve a knowledge and understanding of all the values in social capitalism, not just the value of money.

Who are the communicants or receivers? What do they need to know? These are fundamental questions. If people do need a form of training it is not difficult to convert this diffuse need into a more conscious 'wanting', thus supplying the motivational purpose necessary for any effective training.

3. *The Situation*

Perhaps the most crucial factor in the situation is the time available. It is obviously possible to adopt a more ambitious strategy if you have mature students on a one-year course. The trend in management education (and professional training in general) is towards shorter formal courses and longer periods of learning 'on the job'. But even so the time which can be devoted to the practical thinking seminars will vary considerably. It is an obvious common sense rule not to bite off more than can be safely chewed in the duration of a course or programme.

There may also be some unique features in the situation which either favour or hinder the further exploration of the valuing element to managerial judgement. A particular chairman or managing director, for example, may be especially aware of the importance of the topic. A business school based at a university is in a situation where it should be natural for it to investigate the value dimensions of management studies.

4. *The Communicator*

The difficulty of finding teachers equipped by temperament, experience and knowledge to guide any of the more ambitious expeditions into the hinterland of value thinking has been noted by American writers in the past twenty years or more.

The person qualified in two or more disciplines and with experience of the manager's world will probably be found in a university. But the university-based business schools are responsible for only a small percentage of the total of those undergoing management training at any one time. Thus it is important that these few individuals and their host business schools should share their 'know-how' with those many other trainers in other educational centres and on the staffs of organisations who wish to make this field one of their specialisms. Such learning could be sealed by the granting of a diploma or even a higher degree if pursued systematically and under proper supervision. But a series of one week 'workshops' would probably meet the needs of many training managers who wish to introduce a further degree of ethical discussion, beyond the general awareness of valuing and values which should be a product of the bread-and-butter training in decisions which they offer.

Doubtless a process of discovery about the scope and range of his own value judgements is part of the communicator's preparation. Especially he needs to know how far and in what ways he differs from the broad social consensus on the priority of value in business which makes possible compromise between the varying interests involved, such as shareholders, employees and the public. If he is to teach at a university level the communicator should also know where he stands in the age-old debate about the origins and nature of value. However sure he may be of his own standing, the communicator has to remain open to in-coming messages, words and ideas which may change his radar-screen picture of values. For it is perhaps those willing to be changed when truth appears from any source who are most likely to bring about change in other people.

5. *The Content*

The possible content of a short two- or three-day course on effective thinking, decision-making and problem-solving, I have already described fully in *Training for Decisions* (1971). The earlier sessions in such a course would naturally introduce the concepts of valuing and values.

On this basic framework, however, it is possible to build extra sessions on the values of social capitalism and moral judgement, according to the needs or requirements of the course members. If we assume, for example, a one-month residential programme for post-graduate-level managers in their thirties and early forties, then perhaps a whole day should be spent on the valuing aspects of decision-making. This day could be either encapsulated within an extended decision-making course of four or five days, or else seen as a free-standing day designed to follow the course some weeks later, both to recapitulate its main points and to develop further one of its main themes.

Each one of us has to construct our own philosophy. Management training or education should make available for individual study and digestion the company, trade and professional sets of ethics. Moreover, management courses should provide some opportunities for practising the application of them to some problematic situations.

Therefore the content of courses on valuing in the moral and social fields should include:

1. the exploration and mapping of values
2. the study of the existing and relevant codes of ethics
3. the teaching that both 1 and 2 are necessary for finding solutions in problem situations where time is limited.

Naturally this content will be enriched if cross-reference is made to other subjects in the syllabus, such as the behavioural sciences, and business history. The latter, a much neglected study, might well include the evolution of social responsibility, business ethics and management education itself (with its own distinctive academic values) in the past century.

6. *Methods*

The methods of education chosen should conform to the general participative and practical approach. In other words, lectures or monologues should be kept to the minimum and the emphasis should be on learning through discussion and discovery. The tutor in this aspect of decision-making has to steer a careful course between 'preaching sermons' on the one hand and compounding confusion, doubt and uncertainty on the other. His skill will lie in utilising the tides and winds of good educational methods.

Much advocacy for the use of case studies or histories in this field has already been made, so that the advantages of posing a concrete situation to students requires no further elaboration from me. But the point needs to be reiterated that case studies do not teach anything by themselves. For learning depends upon the interplay of experience and principles, or practice and theory. Case studies provide only second-hand experience in a written form; the general ideas which are illuminated by—or applied to—the case situations are usually distinct and more important.

Filmed case studies could be exceptionally useful in this context. Such films might be especially prepared for management education on a world-wide basis. Like the Royal Canadian Air Force film *Integrity* they could be left 'open-ended' to promote discussion on the situation depicted. Additionally (or alternatively), existing entertainment films and management training films could be combed for possible twenty-minute extracts suitable for exposing the moral dimensions in decision-making by individuals, groups, companies or organisations.

All the possible methods—discussions, talks, written material, visual aids, case studies and films—need to be integrated, so that there is an aesthetically pleasing variety about the seminar, be it one-day or less. For the tutor has to stimulate the interest of the course members not least by the use of different training methods.

CONCLUSION

It would be unwarranted to claim that management education can make more than a modest contribution to the overall development of social capitalism. Early frames of family life, one's natural disposition, the quality of education from play-group to university or college, the lives and examples of the men and women, and the slow influence of personal philosophy or religion: all these factors play larger parts in forming the mind and spirit of any manager. But a good teacher can help managers to become generally aware of their values and to compare them with the consensus of value judgements in a particular company, industry or profession. Possibly doors may be opened for further reflection and personal growth. You cannot teach an ethical awareness—it can only be learnt.

CHAPTER 9

The Role of the Company Board

In the industrial and commercial field the characteristic organisation is the joint-stock company, owned by shareholders and managed on their behalf by a range of employees. The latter can be roughly categorised according to the functions they perform. There is an appointed leader, known variously as the chairman or president, managing director or vice-president. He has a board of directors, whose role is made up of several basic functions.

The chief of these functions is to contribute towards the formulation of policy: the longer-term answers to the question, 'What shall we do next?' In general terms policy is the course of action which people pursue in order to achieve their ends. It follows that the board should be as clear as possible about those ends. The assumption that such a consensus over values already exists may be true, but it needs to be tested at intervals. In a socialist capitalist society, however, the board will increasingly tend to envisage the purpose of the company as embracing not only the common task of producing a particular goods or service in such a way as to provide a return on capital satisfactory to the shareholders, but also as providing continuing and better employment for their fellow employees. There is no essential conflict between these aims, but there is an underlying tension between them which may erupt into conflicts of interest. It has been predicted, for example, that by the year 2000 world trade will probably increase to fifteen times its present volume but in so doing will employ only two per cent more people. Doubtless the pressures to avert this prospect of massive unemployment will grow rapidly in the next decade, and will stand high in the list of social factors which must be taken into account in the formulation of business policy at board level.

A second major area of leadership responsibility, which necessarily involves the board, is the maintenance and growth of the organisation. Beyond the survival needs, which come to the fore when the situation turns threatening, these maintenance necessities include such activities as the achieving of a balance with the competition in the environment (not too much, not too little), the provision of executive leaders, the progressive amendment of the organisational structure, and the setting and preservation of standards of conduct and practice. In one way or other this organisational maintenance revolves around the perennial issue of the best relation of parts to a whole. The standing organisational question is how best to achieve the unified action of the whole without impairing or destroying the vitality of the parts. It is a constant search for the elusive ideal of a corporate integrity in a fast changing environment, an organisation which is characterised by speed of response, grace and flexibility as well as by strength, mass and weight.

A vital aspect of this social cohesiveness of any organisation concerns such unseen realities as philosophy, morale and morality. Consequently the board cannot escape responsibility for these facets of any common enterprise. All long-standing groups or organisations develop not only a group personality but also an ethos or character which normally includes a more or less implicit code of ethics. These ethics are the corporate answers, however provisional, to the questions What is right? and What is wrong? The answers will rarely be stated in written formulas or verbal rules: more usually they are purveyed in the commonly accepted practices, unspoken traditions or even the mixtures of myths and facts which make up the group's tradition as opposed to its actual history.

Boards of directors continually face the necessity of reconciling or arbitrating between the three sets or clusters of values: the values of the common task (quality, efficiency, finance); the values of individual employees (work, security, money); the values of corporate unity (industry, group, company), all in relation to the whole living, changing, moving environment of society and nature. These sets of values sail in harmony when viewed from a distance, but close up they creak and groan at daily tension with each other. Thus boards contribute to the satisfactory progress of the company, both in the short- and long-term by selecting the chief executive and sacking him if necessary, supporting and advising him to the best of their ability, and sharing fully in his responsibility for establishing the corporate ethos of the company.

THE NEED FOR MORE RESEARCH

Despite a spring-tide in management education, supported by large grants of money for research, it is strange that boards of directors—the seats of authority for the direction and control of a business—have been largely neglected by researchers.

How far does the British boardroom differ from its American counterpart? Considerably, if we are to believe a book written by Myles L. Mace and published in 1971 under the title of *Directors: Myth and Reality*. According to the author, it is a *myth* that boards of directors fulfil these functions: 'to establish broad objectives and policies, to ask discerning questions, and to select the chief executive'—and it is a *myth* that the outside directors are chosen because they are qualified to do so. The *reality* is that they are selected because they are friends of the company's president or because their names have a prestige value. The inside directors are appointed for such dubious reasons as to retain the services of an executive who might otherwise leave the company. Apparently these executives rarely speak at board meetings for fear of embarrassing the president before these distinguished or powerful outside directors. The board contributes little to the three functions listed above, except in a crisis such as the sudden death of the president before he has named his successor. If the president himself is unsatisfactory it is customary for the board members—not the president—to tender their resignations.

Besides its emergency role in a succession crisis, or in such matters as aiding the departure of relatives from family businesses, the board does also have a positive function as a kind of 'corporate conscience'. It also ensures that shareholders do receive periodic reports on the progress of the company. Yet in reality the functions for which boards exist are not well fulfilled.

These conclusions rest upon research methods which will not commend themselves to the purists. Yet all those who have objectively studied the reality of boardroom practice as against the ideal, however defined by lawyers, custom or organisational theorists, conclude that there is much room for improvement in every area of its activity. It would be surprising if that conclusion was otherwise—and perhaps rather alarming if it was. For top management would then have no incentive for self-improvement. And a complacent board of directors would not expect the main body of employees to respond to its call for better results when set such a bad example itself.

Within this general scope for improvement lies the vital if background function of being the corporate conscience of the company (understanding conscience as the forward-looking radar-beam rather than the retrospective judge). Without the general will to generate better decisions in the boardroom, however, the senior, middle and junior levels of management—and the shop-floor as well—may gaze upwards and declare, doubtless in more forceful language than Shakespeare: 'Do not, like some ungracious pastors do, show us the steep and thorny way to heaven, while they themselves the primrose path of dalliance tread, and reck not their own rede.'

SOCIAL RESPONSIBILITY

The evidence suggests that many company boards of directors have responded to the challenge or necessity of the times, and now seriously take into account the change of values in the past seventy years which has been recorded in the first part of this book. The value placed on money has not lost ground in consequence. Indeed it is the high value placed on money together with the high value on the human person, as individual and as member of society, which constitutes the system named here social capitalism. It is not so much that boards of directors are unaware of the growth or disclosure of the human values, but that they experience difficulty in determining the weightings of the less-quantifiable factors in their business decisions.

These generalisations are supported by the findings in a study of fifteen very large British companies, undertaken by Barbara Shenfield and published in 1971 under the title of *Company Boards: Their Responsibilities to Shareholders, Employees and the Community*. Only one managing director defined his purpose solely in terms of making money for the shareholders: the remainder professed to incorporate in their purposes the collection of concerns currently known as 'social responsibility'. These they perceived, in the main, as employee welfare, company philanthropy, deferring to the public interest (on, for instance, pollution, location, pricing), and the development of a more democratic style of management.

The companies surveyed were in no doubt that their primary aim was to be profitable. They saw social responsibility as consistent with profitability, at least in the long run. This conviction, based doubtless on experience, leaves open the question of motive, which enters into any discussion of morality. For the reasons which people give in public for being—or seeking—the good may be as much conscious or unconscious rationalisation as the plausible reasons they use to justify selfish action. Thus it is easy for an observer to be misled by confusing *motives* on which an action is based (given usually in the form of reasons), and *rationalisations* adopted to communicate, persuade or justify a decision already taken on other grounds. Mrs Shenfield may tell us more about these *post-facto* verbalisations than pure motives when she observes that 'The greater part of the policies described by companies as ways of meeting what they conceived to be their social responsibilities was in fact founded on enlightened self-interest.' We should not focus too much on the 'self' and ignore the 'light' in her remark. Money is the *lingua franca* of business, reflecting its traditional but much-questioned role as a universal yardstick of value. Therefore it is not surprising if directors resort to it in justifying decisions which may have more than one root in the depth mind of the individual manager or company.

Mrs Shenfield's study demonstrates with much clarity that when a board of directors is resolved to take seriously the interests of employees and the community as well as those of the shareholders and customers they are only on the threshold of the matter. The difficulties of implementing the purpose and spirit of social capitalism are considerable, and show signs of growing harder in some ways, while at the same time growing easier in other respects.

Mrs Shenfield adduces evidence which supports some of the conclusions of the Baumhart and Webley surveys discussed in Chapter 7. For example, she found that twelve of the fifteen company boards had on occasions accepted the financial consequences of keeping on employees who had outlived their usefulness to the company for one reason or another. But she also demonstrates well how much more complex is reality than those gutted-and-filleted 'situations' dished up by the business ethics surveys. Her four major case studies, in which these difficulties are explored, concern respectively employment practices, charitable donations, the public interest (consumer protection through government intervention overpricing in the chemical industry), and participative management.

The most important and most intriguing of these case studies concerns a construction company which introduced a system of more permanent jobs for its work force on building sites. The board believed that providing such continuity would add profitability by attracting and retaining a better calibre of work people and ensure a long-term supply of skilled labour. At the same time the management also acted in what they conceived to be the best interests of the individual employees. Consequently, it introduced such 'good industrial practices' as better site amenities and contributory pension schemes. This policy proved difficult to implement, however, because it was the very 'casual labour' nature of that industry, with its ingredients of a particular pay system, options over travel and variety, which had attracted the bulk of the work force in the first place. Those most interested in permanent employment were older men and coloured immigrants. But if only the company had embraced it the scheme would certainly have led to reduced profitability.

Thus the little empirical research available does suggest that boards of directors in both British and American companies are growing more aware of their social responsibility bundle of concerns, and that they seek to take them into account when formulating policies. But case studies reveal that they are likely to encounter unexpected difficulties when they make and implement decisions within this wider frame of reference. Doubtless these teething pains of social capitalism are sufficiently sharp to provide an excuse for the weaker brethren to withdraw once more behind the portcullis of the balance sheet. Moreover, these problems have provided sufficient disincentive to ensure that the march of progress in the vast majority of businesses resembles more the annual inching forwards of an ice glacier than the joyful rush of a mountain stream. The more impatient spirits, those 'hawks' of social responsibility, have proposed methods of making certain that company boards do take more seriously values and interests other than money and profit into consideration. These proposed remedies must now be considered in turn.

REVISION OF COMPANY LAW

Perhaps the most widely canvassed method is a revision of the Companies Act (1948), which defines the legal duties of a director in a joint-stock enterprise solely in terms of his obligations to the company, thus:

The Role of the Company Board

The business of the Company shall be managed by the directors, who may pay all expenses incurred in promoting and registering the Company, and may exercise all such powers of the Company as are not (by the Act or by these regulations) required to be exercised by the Company in General Meeting, subject, nevertheless, to any of these regulations, to the provisions of the Act and to such regulations, being not inconsistent with the aforesaid regulations or provisions, as may be presented by the Company in General Meeting.

But no regulation made by the Company in General Meeting shall invalidate any prior act of the directors which would have been valid if that regulation had not been made.

(Article 80, Table A, Schedule I)

The wording of these clauses, it is argued, should be altered to embrace responsibilities towards the community at large, the employees and the customer. Some also question the moral implications of the concept of limited liability, as first embodied legally in the Companies Act (1856), but this theme is a secondary one.

A new Companies Bill is currently being prepared, and will come before Parliament in 1974. Doubtless the politicians and lawyers will study to bring the proposed Bill into line with the practice of the European Economic Community. In particular, they will have to weigh the advantages of different solutions to the problem of board composition, and especially the role, nature and numbers of non-executive directors. Whatever their solutions to these problems should they add some new clauses making it legally mandatory for company boards to take into account all the values and interests of social capitalism?

Many observers have come out against the efficacy of such a legal innovation. Mrs Barbara Shenfield, for example, in her book already quoted, rejected legislation as a method of ensuring that companies fulfilled their social responsibilities. She concluded that stronger social pressures from organised labour, alert customer associations and the growing weight of public opinion would be more successful in bringing about improvements in the broader spectrum of industrial, commercial and financial companies.

From the Company Law Reform White Paper of 1973 it is clear that the Companies Act (1974) will probably include a statement of the social and public responsibilities of the board of directors. This would be welcome if only as a protection for directors against any claim by shareholders seeking compensation for loss caused by directors' actions not taken directly and solely in the shareholders' interests. But the legislators have put most of their trust in a mandatory fuller disclosure of information, holding that 'openness in company affairs is the first principle in securing responsible behaviour'. By thus widening the scope of the information which must be disclosed by law the government obviously hopes that companies will come increasingly under social pressures to act according to the total value system of social capitalism.

A CODE OF CORPORATE CONDUCT

In January 1973 the Company Affairs Committee of the Confederation of British Industry, chaired by Lord Watkinson, produced an interim report entitled *A New Look at the Responsibilities of the British Public Company*. The Committee recommended that a code of corporate conduct would be a guide to directors in 'making decisions with a social or ethical content; to provide them with a body of doctrine and to help raise the general standard of corporate behaviour'. The status of a code should be 'advisory' rather than 'mandatory'. A panel representing the CBI, investors and other City interests would be responsible for updating it.

Some critics of the proposal, holding that good company boards need no code while bad ones would ignore or break it with impunity, placed their trust in the general standards of society and in the personal ethics of individuals. But we have seen that professional codes are useful not as alternatives to social and personal values and rules, but as complementary to them. Thus the proposed Code of Corporate Conduct should concentrate upon the recurring general situations or problems which face boards of directors as a whole, and not merely reiterate in abstract language the values of social capitalism. Such a code would therefore have to rest upon a considerable amount of research into the agendas and actual discussions of boards, and it would have to be systematically updated as both business and society evolve.

On the assumption that some kind of representative body would be needed to relate the code to practice, what should its status be? If we reject the nightmare of a Star Chamber with full inquisitional powers we are left with two options: bodies of quasi-legal or non-legal status.

The arguments for a non-legal status are both practical and moral. Any kind of legally sanctioned code would be difficult if not impossible to apply in practice: the attempt would bring both the law and the quasi-legal panel or committee into disrepute. On moral grounds, any self-discipline is better than any imposed discipline, and therefore to be preferred in this field. Behind this reasoning we may perhaps trace also a traditional distaste for the intervention of the law, even in the sheep's clothing of a representative panel of directors, and a fear of the bureaucratic consequences which might go with it.

In this context the history of the City Take-over Panel is illuminating. Set up in the mid 1960s as a result of what *The Times* has called 'the public outcry over a particularly black period of chaotic banditry on the company take-over scene', the Panel on Take-overs and Mergers was established by the City as a preferable alternative to a statutory body equivalent to the American Securities and Exchange Commission. The latter can bring civil proceedings and act through powerful instruments such as injunctions, but it had acquired in Britain an unenviable reputation for being a cumbersome bureaucracy. In February 1971, the Financial Editor of *The Times* reviewed the progress of the Take-over Panel thus:

The decision to opt for the freedom of self-regulation has been triumphantly justified.

But the panel's success in its specialised task, by showing that regulation could work, has underlined the inadequacies of much of

153

the rest of our regulation of company and stock exchange practice. Fraud, insurance company collapses, accounting irregularities and the massive failure to enforce the disclosure of information required in the Companies Acts, manipulation of shares, and the ability of rogue company operators to fleece outside shareholders over a long period have all—like insider trading itself—been put in sharper focus.

We have seen that the theoretical recourse to the civil law gives shareholders (let alone policy or deposit holders) no real protection. We have seen how the Department of Trade and Industry's regulatory departments, neglected and understaffed, have interpreted their role narrowly and failed to do their job. The Fraud Squad, hampered by lack of co-operation and co-ordination, especially with the regulatory bodies, has been a sword of vengeance with a limited success ratio rather than a protector. And as the insider trading problem demonstrates once again, the Stock Exchange Council and the Take-over Panel, though well informed and frequently on the ball, have by their nature few powers to protect the shareholder. Unless the miscreants are merchant banks or stockbrokers, the only real power is often to suspend a share quotation, which harms the shareholders in need of care and protection more than anyone.

One possible solution was to turn the Take-over Panel into a quasi-legal body. Clearly this possibility has been seriously considered, for *The Times* on 25 May 1971 reported that Lord Shawcross, the chairman of the Panel, had said that the existing legal machinery was inadequate for dealing with the abuse of inside information in share dealings and other misconduct by directors of public companies.

Introducing the panel's annual report for the year to the end of last March (1971), Lord Shawcross said that although the panel still held the view that the abuse of inside information was a rare occurrence, there were occasions, investigating share dealings by directors, when the panel would have liked legal powers to demand documents and take evidence from witnesses under oath. . . . And commenting on the report he added that the machinery of companies' legislation needs to be revitalised and speeded up.

154

The Role of the Company Board

Although Lord Shawcross stressed yesterday that the voluntary system which allows the panel to operate in the City is preferable and more effective than the establishment of a legal bureaucracy like the American Securities & Exchange Commission, he would like to see the panel put on a quasi-legal basis.

'I sometimes look,' he said, 'rather enviously at the General Medical Council, a statutory body established by charter with the right to question witnesses.' Lord Shawcross added, as a personal opinion, that he thought it would be a good thing if, given safeguards to protect the rights of individuals, the panel were given a similar official charter.

In February 1973, however, Lord Shawcross proposed another course of action. The City Take-over Panel and Stock Exchange advised the Government that 'insider dealings' (using confidential information gained as a result of a professional position with a company, or from someone in that position, to make a profit by dealing in shares) should henceforth—in the interests of the shareholders—be made a criminal offence. In other words, the Panel retains its status and advantages as a non-legal body, but is able to stimulate accurate and effective revisions of the law to deal with particular actions which offend the consensus of business morality.

In July 1973 the Company Law Reform White Paper duly appeared with a promise that insider dealings would be made a criminal offence in the Companies Act (1974). Commentators were not slow to point out that the White Paper had neither adequately defined insider dealings, nor shown how the malpractice could be effectively stamped out. Yet we should not be distracted from contemplating this emerging general pattern of regulation by the particular difficulties of defining insider dealings adequately, or catching the cunning evaders. It can be hard for judges to distinguish cases of rape from forceful seductions, nor are rapists easy to catch, but all that does not deter us from making rape a criminal offence.

The campaign against insider dealings is essentially directed at individual black or off-white sheep. The panel responsible for the

Code of Corporate Practice, however, would primarily be concerned with the board of directors as a group. The minimum standards of right conduct expected of a board should be reflected in the law of the land, especially in the proposed revision of company law. By the nature of law, these standards should be enforceable in some way; it should be possible to prove when they have been infringed and to state the appropriate penalties.

Yet morality is not identical with the law. A Code of Corporate Practice would define the consensus of moral practice in social capitalism either beyond the present tide-marks of law or else in areas which by their nature are not legally enforceable. But the danger of such a code is that it lacks authority, and may be soon forgotten as just another piece of paper. A possible remedy would be to utilise a declaratory function in the law without invoking its compulsory or punitive function. Thus the code would be attached to a new Companies Act, bathed in the aura of legality, but it would be almost entirely 'advisory'.

Two analogies for this course would be the Highway Code and the Industrial Relations Code of Practice. The latter, for example, is attached to the Industrial Relations Act (1971). The purpose of this Code was stated as: 'to give practical guidance for promoting good industrial relations', and it set out to do so in accordance with the four general principles of the Act: freely conducted collective bargaining, orderly procedures for settling disputes, free association of workers and employers, and freedom and security for workers. The Code imposes no legal obligations and failure to observe its recommended practices does not by itself render anyone liable to prosecution. But Section Four of the Industrial Relations Act does state that the relevant provisions of the Code should be taken into account in any legal proceedings under the Act in the National Industrial Relations Court or an industrial tribunal.

As a preliminary step, before embarking on a similar venture with the Companies Act of 1974 or subsequent company legislation later in the decade, it would be important that there should be some research into the effects of the Industrial Relations Code of

Practice. If it were possible to reproduce the simple, clear and practical language of the exemplary 1971 Code of Practice in the much more difficult field of morality, then a Code of Corporate Conduct would be a welcome annexe to a Companies Act in the 1970s.

There remains the difficult problem of sanctions—or the lack of them—to daunt the legislators of social capitalism. While admitting that 'a Code of Conduct might be appropriate' the authors of the government's Company Law Reform White Paper clearly doubted its practicality:

> For a Code to be effective in that area of responsibility which this Paper has described as 'social' or 'moral'—and given that by its nature much of the material cannot be put in specific and precise form—*some independent source of judgment may be necessary*. The Take-Over Panel suggests a precedent, but the Panel has of course the sanctions of the Stock Exchange behind it, and it is not at present easy to see what counterpart might exist in relation to the general run of industrial decisions.

In contrast, the framers of the Companies Act (1974) are pinning all their substantial hopes on securing fuller disclosure. 'The Government's general approach,' declares the White Paper, 'is that disclosure of information is the best guarantee of fair dealing and the best antidote to mistrust'.

The government, however, has left unanswered the issue of just how the legal gaps, social questions and moral problems, inevitably to be exposed by the fuller spate of information in directors' reports, are to be dealt with in a satisfactory way. A larger staff of inspectors in the Department of Trade and Industry is obviously not the complete answer. And so we return to the need for a Code of Corporate Conduct, appended to the new Act or its successor, and monitored by a representative panel of company directors and others.

The representative panel responsible for the Code, possibly drawn from such bodies as the CBI, the Association of British Chambers of Commerce, the Retail Consortium, and the Chamber of Shipping augmented by others chosen from the wider community, might have five functions:

1. To communicate the Code to all boards of directors and to each new director of a publicly-quoted company; and to promote discussion and to generate research on its guide-lines.
2. To serve as an advisory body to company boards who find themselves faced with an especially testing moral dilemma or series of value conflicts.
3. To inquire into the circumstances when individual directors resign from boards on grounds of conscience and wish to have their reputations vindicated.
4. To provide swift and accurate feedback to the government on the needs for further revisions of the corpus of laws touching upon the conduct of company boards.
5. To update the Code of Corporate Conduct so that it remains ahead of the minimal morality enshrined in law but in keeping with the practice of the better company boards.

The major sanction for a Code of Corporate Practice, as for any other group code, is the social pressures of one's professional peers. Therefore the only powers which a panel need possess is the right to make public examples of good practice or bad practice. And that right is best granted and exercised through representative bodies such as the Confederation of British Industry. At its heart lies the responsible collection and routing of *information* about the decisions of boards of directors. But the panel need not act on that information itself: rather that body may merely help to ensure that the right party receives and digests the information. That party or parties might be such people as shareholders of the company in question, the Director-General of Fair Trading (appointed under the provisions of the Fair Trading Act of 1973), or those committees of Parliament responsible for revising company law. Thus the role of the panel, using the Code of Corporate Practice as its frame of reference, would be one of subtle, flexible and well-informed surveillance.

The Role of the Company Board

Yet it would be unwise to entertain too great an expectation from the framing and acceptance of such a code for company boards, and its arrival on the Statute Book in 'advisory' clothes. Many people have fashionably blamed the relative ineffectiveness of previous codes and statements upon their lack of teeth, either in the form of an apparatus of councils, committees and professional qualifications, or in the guise of legal or quasi-legal punishments. But the real difficulty about any code is that it remains obstinately *external* to all but those who have actually had a hand in formulating its specific provisions. It is only the law-makers who have the law written on their hearts.

CHANGES IN BOARD COMPOSITION

One characteristic of many company boards is the presence of non-executive directors. A growing number of observers have suggested that in a widening and developing of the concept of the non-executive director there lies the true hope for ensuring that the social aspects of decisions and policies are taken into account. In contrast to the externalism of law or quasi-legal codes, this method promises to infiltrate the board with a 'fifth column' of socially-minded and ethically-alert directors. The case for an extension of the proportion of non-executive directors on boards has been largely argued in terms of traditional capitalism, namely that they are the best guarantors of the shareholders' interests *vis-à-vis* the management. But the proposals for worker directors and public interest directors rely much more upon the value system of social capitalism for their cogency. The established presence of the two-tier board, already complete with worker directors, in the Common Market countries has thrown the issue into high relief for the government of Britain, which might be in danger of finding itself out of step with its EEC partners in the current move towards a European Company Statute.

The constitutional merits of the one board composed of executive and non-executive directors (Britain, America) and the division into two boards, one in the supervisory role and the other charged with running the company (Germany, Holland, Norway), can be debated endlessly. As the German model could well be officially adopted by the European Economic Community doubtless much discussion and research will continue to revolve around the question. In microcosm it reflects the much larger constitutional issue of whether it is better to divide the legislative and executive functions (America) or to keep them together as in the British parliamentary system. Again the opposition to the introduction of any form of mandatory two-tier board structure by Lord Watkinson's Committee in 1973 may be taken as broadly representative of the British attitude: 'The existence of a supervisory board must take away from the members of the management board that feeling of ultimate and total responsibility which should be the most compelling influence towards effective management.'

Under the two-tier system the supervisory board appoints the executive board. In the German coal and steel companies these supervisory boards (the *Aufsichtsrat*) consist of equal numbers of shareholders' and workers' representatives, with one member who is a spokesman for neither camp. The workers can also recommend or veto the appointment of one member of the executive board (the *Vorstand*), a right first introduced during the Allied occupation and subsequently confirmed by law. Other German companies however, maintain a two-to-one ratio in favour of shareholders' directors on the supervisory board. In the Netherlands, where the unions disliked the minority role assigned to labour in the German system while the Dutch legislative also wanted to avoid its implicit danger of a polarisation of interests, the law allows both the works council and the assembly of shareholders to nominate or veto all appointments to supervisory directorships, but making actual selection the result of co-option by the board—an interesting mixture of the democratic and oligarchic methods of perpetuation.

The German and Dutch systems assume the role of works councils as the constituency which does the electing, nominating or vetoing on behalf of the labour force. The acceptance of works councils in post-war Europe rested largely upon the belief that they had proved themselves in Britain in the 1930s and 1940s. Yet the history of industrial relations in Britain since 1945 has seen an emphasis upon the role of trade unions and a corresponding lack of emphasis upon the works council, although many survive and a few flourish as a means of upward communication and consultation.

So far British industry has looked askance at the worker director aspect of European industrial democracy. Employers' federations, for example, have long entertained the fear that the institution of worker directors on the main company board would enter a Trojan Horse into the boardroom concealing all manner of militant and politically-extreme trade unionists. These worker directors would study confidential information and make use of it to sharpen their pay claims or to take early industrial action against possible redundancies. Moreover, it is sometimes claimed, the particular pattern of widespread shareholding in Britain—in contrast to the effective control of most continental companies by a few big institutions or families—render British firms much more liable to take-over bids, and the presence of worker nominees on the board would enlarge the danger of the 'leakage' of information. Obviously this latter argument is secondary to the major one about pay claims and redundancies. In the concept of industry as divided into 'two sides' it remains fatally unclear to all concerned where the loyalties of the worker director should be.

For their part, until very recently, the leaders of the British trades union movement have been equally opposed towards the concept of the worker director. Left-wingers have regarded such an arrangement as an open acceptance of the permanence of the capitalist system, while right-wingers viewed it as a revival of the old liberal idea of co-partnership in place of the traditional separate stance of the unions as one embattled 'side' in industry, which they held to be much better suited for the real work of wage bargaining. Thus, for very different reasons, British management and unions for long agreed in disliking the concept of worker participation at board level, while both remained unwilling to

K*

commit themselves irrevocably against it for all time. Lord Watkinson's Committee, for example, pinned their faith in better communication, consultation and a proper negotiating machinery as the British method of fully involving employees in decisions which affect their working lives.

Whether or not these particular attitudes and policies of British senior management and labour leaders can survive Britain's entry into the European *milieu* of social capitalism is another matter.

By the summer of 1973 some leaders in the trade union movement had already revoked their earlier opinions on the issue, and laid claim to an extravagant number of boardroom places for worker directors. They also began to explore ways of reconciling the continental model of the works council as the constitutional electors of the worker directors with the existing British structures of trade union organisation at company and factory level. So far, however, the willingness of politicians and some trade union leaders to consider changes in company law in respect of worker directors, in keeping with possible developments in the EEC, has not been reciprocated by the general body of senior managers nor by many union leaders. Doubtless there will eventually be a British compromise, but even its broad outline remains entirely uncertain at present, and it will only emerge towards the end of the 1970s after much more debate, research and experiment.

If some directors are to speak primarily for the shareholders and others for the employees, why not directors appointed to advise on the social policy of the company? This proposal may seem impractical, yet in 1971 the largest company in the world, General Motors, elected to its main board a coloured Baptist pastor, Dr Leon H. Sullivan. Besides holding a master's degree in religion from Columbia University and gaining experience of finance as a board member of the Girard Trust Bank in Philadelphia, Dr Sullivan had achieved note as the founder of the Opportunities Industrialisation Centres of America, whose 60 or more branches promote industrial training for coloured people. As James M. Roche, Chairman of General Motors, declared: 'Dr Sullivan has a distinguished record of service to his community and is the type of person who can bring to our board the benefit of his knowledge and expertise in the areas of public concern.' It would be interesting to discover how many other companies in America had followed the lead of General Motors and appointed a non-executive director to represent the 'public concern'.

The main argument against public interest directors drawn from outside the world of business is that they would lack the practical experience which must inform moral judgement in working situations. Technical and moral issues do not come neatly separated, but in complex mixtures. Therefore a considerable amount of first-hand experience and background knowledge of business should characterise the non-executive director. As for the moral concern, that is the responsibility of the whole board and each individual director, conscience cannot be delegated, even to a bishop.

A chairman of a company should ensure that there always are men or women of exceptional integrity and long experience, who can be relied upon to raise moral issues or stir up latent ethical awareness of their colleagues. Such a person or persons may be executive or non-executive directors, for the quality of their contribution depends more on character than any other factor. A small group needs someone to articulate its moral conscience. A board of directors may not want to hear a particular message, but if it comes from a director who personifies the qualities and achievements of a good businessman, the board will listen.

Thus it becomes clear that social capitalism calls above all for wisdom in the boardroom. 'It is a curious thing,' wrote Lord Attlee in 1964, 'that nearly every Cabinet throws up at least one man, whether he is a departmental Minister or not, of whom a newcomer may ask: "What is *he* doing here?" He is there because he is wise. You will hear a junior Cabinet Minister being told by the Prime Minister, perhaps, "If you are going to do that, you would be well advised to have a talk with X".' Who can doubt that boards of directors will need such wise counsellors if they are to incorporate into their decisions such factors as the status of their employees as ends as well as means, the needs of society as a whole (and particularly those communities where their facilities are located), the various interests of the shareholders, bankers, customers, competitors and suppliers, and the conservation of natural resources.

SHAREHOLDER PARTICIPATION

It is often assumed that the interests of shareholders are diametrically opposed to the non-monetary values of social capitalism. The shareholders are regarded as the Old Guard of capitalism, interested only in their dividends. But such a belief ignores the character of social capitalism as a social as well as an economic phenomenon. The shareholders are members of society more immediately than they are members of the company using their money. Therefore they could exert a considerable influence on a company board to take more into account than all the values held to be ends in our world society.

'Our Thalidomide Children': A Case Study

The story of the part played by shareholders in the dealings of the Distillers Company with parents of the thalidomide children is instructive. The value of some of the weakest individuals in our society, handicapped children, was placed against the profits of a company which for one reason or another had resolved to accept the definition of its moral obligation as determined in the law courts. By the end of 1972 seven years of legal wrangling had already passed, with a total of £1 million awarded to some of the children, and the Distillers Company had on offer to the parents of the 342 thalidomide children £5 million, which would amount to £11,850,000 in ten years with tax concessions.

As background, it is worth recording that the Distillers Company's profits for the year ending 31 March 1972 were £62,190,000 and their assets were valued at £247 million. The salaries of the 17 directors amounted that year to £303,000—an average of

£18,000 a man. Large institutional shareholders held one-third of Distillers' issued stock of £181,584,722 in 50p shares. They included several large insurance firms, such as the Prudential Assurance (9,184,738 shares), and pension funds (British Petroleum, 3,121,877 shares), besides Liverpool, Kensington, Chelsea, York, Durham and Essex councils and many others. In all there were 250,000 shareholders.

Throughout December 1972 social pressures mounted against the Distillers Company for their delay in improving on the £5 million offer. The concerted campaign began to produce tangible results, reflected in dipping share prices. Early in January 1973 the Wrenson chain of 260 stores announced that they would boycott Distillers' products, of which they sold some £500,000 a year. Then a spokesman for Fine Fare, which has 1,000 supermarkets and stores throughout Britain, said: 'We are aware of the feelings of what must be a large proportion of our customers on the subject and we won't go out of our way to promote Distillers' products.'

American consumer champion Ralph Nader entered the fray, threatening a new era of prohibition in America against such Distillers' exports as Haig, Johnny Walker and White Horse whisky, Booth's and Gordon's gin, Cossack vodka, Pimms No. 1 Cup and Hine cognac. York City Council and Durham County Council now were reported as joining in the call for an extraordinary Annual General Meeting of Distillers to seek ways of gaining more compensation for the 342 children.

On 3 January 1973 the market value of Distillers fell by £9 million as a result of the growing pressure to provide more compensation for the children. Next day the major industrial shareholders met in London, sharing a common desire to persuade the board to reach a swift, just and satisfactory solution. The seventeen directors of the Distillers Company board came together the day after, and announced shortly afterwards a new offer of £20 million to the thalidomide children.

The institutional shareholders doubtless acted mainly for

financial motives. After all, they were accountable for the funds entrusted to them by a host of individuals throughout society. Yet we cannot lightly assume that they also were not disturbed also by the moral dimension of the matter. Whatever their motives it is significant that these institutional investors were both able and willing to act so powerfully in the situation as a catalyst of change.

These corporate bodies, however, could not have played their part unless the value of the children as ends entirely precious had not been stirred, along with the social sense that they are part of us —'our thalidomide children' as *The Times* leader called them. Besides the parents of the children, members of Parliament and various charitable trusts, a significant contribution to the campaign had come from a small group acting from moral motives and known as the Distillers Company Shareholders Action Committee. On 3 January the *Evening Standard* gave this interesting account of its origins:

> The escalating success story of the dissident Distillers Company shareholders, who are pressing for a fair settlement for the thalidomide victims, was born from very modest beginnings.
>
> The ginger group of stockholders was started and is led by Mrs Sarah Broad, a 37-year-old mother of three with a modest 2,600 shares, inherited from her mother, in the 360 million share company.
>
> From the quiet of her home in Bayswater, where five private shareholders met a few weeks ago, has grown the massive, blossoming support of some of the largest institutions, trade unions and local council shareholders.
>
> But while Mrs Broad initiated this David and Goliath struggle, its launch was considerably more than the simple cry of a shocked housewife.
>
> I learn that her husband, Roger Broad, has been Press Officer for the London office of the EEC for eight-and-a-half years, and later this year takes up a new appointment, as liaison officer between the parliaments in Westminster and Strasbourg.
>
> 'I would never have done it without him,' confessed Mrs Broad. 'He reminded me I had the shares, and my reaction was My God, why haven't I sold them? but he then said I could do much more by hanging on to them and getting a pressure group going. And that's

what happened, but I must admit I didn't expect the big institutions to come out before the extraordinary meeting.

'Yes, it has involved an awful lot of work, there have been the school holidays to cope with, and I've got a seven-month-old baby, too. But my husband's been on holiday over Christmas, and my mother-in-law was staying, and they both helped me. One just hopes that things will get sorted out now. It's a good company in other respects.'

The Shareholders Action Group had raised £1,400 needed to obtain the full details of all shareholders, and published the names of them as soon as they were available. This simple stratagem enabled the various friends of the thalidomide children to get to work. Thus *information* was the pebble in the sling of this David among the army of shareholders.

In many ways the case of the Distillers Company is unique. The value issues were overlain with the strong emotions of compassion aroused by the plight of the thalidomide 'victims'. Even so, many letter-writers in the press, in concert with columnists, sprang to the defence of the Distillers Company, pointing our the involvement of the German drug firm inventors, the Government, doctors and hospitals, and even parents in the thalidomide tragedy. The wide public correspondence illustrated what are perhaps inherent traits in social capitalism: on the one hand a dislike of making any one person or small group into a scapegoat for the evils which afflict us; on the other hand, a righteous anger against an apparently mean-spirited legalism and profit-consciousness in the face of human disaster.

The thalidomide case demonstrated that at least some shareholders are moved by more than the profit motive, and can exercise their sense of responsibility in action. A few journalists saw it as the herald of things to come. Peter Wilsher in *The Sunday Times* (7 January 1973) thought it showed 'a belated realisation that, in fact, it is not possible to draw a rigid line between the financial and the social aspects of a great company's business . . . what the present events show is that the big holders are now ready to move in and impose such views, even when a powerful management sees its responsibilities in a much narrower light.' While Robert Jones, writing in *The Times* next morning, related the case to the whole development I have called social capitalism:

> The concept of the professional manager as a man in an essentially non-political and value-free role who makes his decisions in the interest of efficiency is quite inadequate in the present climate. The reality is that many business decisions are a balancing act between the interest of profit maximisation and the complex mixture of personal and social values.

The issue in the thalidomide case was exceptionally clear, and it lent itself to the determined action of a responsible minority of shareholders who saw themselves as part of an essentially good company. While acknowledging with Peter Wilsher that 'this is a path-breaking occasion' we should not underestimate the particular combination of factors which made it all such a unique show of 'shareholder power'. Yet a path has been opened, others will follow; and we owe that general benefit to the quality of our society indirectly to our thalidomide children, and I hope that one day they will understand.

Legal Reforms

In cases less exceptional than the thalidomide tragedy the oligarchic character of many company boards can effectively insulate them against the lighter winds and breezes of shareholder influence. Signs of dissatisfaction with this state of affairs are not hard to come by.

Such matters as the importance of the Annual General Meeting, disclosure of more than the minimum financial information to shareholders and the future of non-voting shares and shares with reduced voting rights are already on the agenda of those committees charged with revising the legislation concerning companies. The object of such reforms should be to make it possible for a shareholder to exercise responsibility for his share in the moral capital of the company. For the old method of selling off shares is losing its appeal to the investor whose conscience is disturbed by the activities of a company.

In order for the voice of the shareholders to be truly effective, however, the board must have a constitution of men and women who are inclined to listen. The most obvious ways of ensuring such openness are placing an age-limit on directors and ensuring that each of them, including the chairman, should be subject to re-election at regular intervals. Lord Watkinson's Committee has proposed that directors should not hold office for more than three years without being compelled to seek re-election. Fully executive directors should retire at sixty-five, and non-executive directors at seventy. All directors aged seventy or over should come up for re-election every year.

The Company Law Reform White Paper reveals an awareness of the importance of the vigilant shareholder, be he an individual or an institution, in the progress of social capitalism. Some technical legal inhibitions on effective shareholder action are noted for reform in 1974, though others still remain for future attention. Yet a 'useful step forward', as the White Paper modestly calls it, will be constituted by the provisions for fuller disclosure of information. Besides extending the range and availability of certain financial data, some of it already required by previous laws, the Companies Act of 1974 may ensure that directors' annual reports include such matters as the performance of their companies in regard to the safety and health of company employees, the number of consumer complaints and what was done about them, and the conduct of industrial relations. 'If shareholders, employees, creditors and the public generally are properly informed,' the White Paper concludes, 'innocent activity will be shown to be so and underhand activity will be inhibited.'

What the shareholders may increasingly want is a 'share' in the moral risks and opportunities of the enterprise quite apart from its financial profit. The shareholder's unique contribution can be made on the basis that he is both a member of society and a member, however tenuously, of the company. The chairman of the board as the chief leader of the whole organisation should make it specifically his business to involve shareholders through better communication to the point where they do feel their membership. Such a company will then draw back an invisible dividend of goodwill from its shareholders.

CONCLUSION

In this chapter four major suggestions for encouraging the boards of companies to accept the unfolding implications of social capitalism have been discussed: revisions of company law; a code of corporate conduct; changes in board composition; and the concept of shareholder participation. Other possibilities, such as 'social audits' and 'ethical consultants', could have lengthened the list except that they either impinge less directly on the boardroom or else belong more to the realm of imaginative thinking than to the art of the possible.

It is the general theme of this book that the progress of social capitalism is taking place slowly and along a very wide front. It is not for us to know where the 'breakthroughs' will come. This conclusion holds true for the cluster of developments or possibilities reviewed in this chapter. Not one of them is the solution by itself; each has a contribution to make towards it. Society can help with advice, support and enabling legislation, but for better or worse the moral leadership of industry and commerce remains firmly in the seats around the boardroom table.

CHAPTER 10

Personal Integrity

'The object of the board is to establish policy and to see that the policy is carried out. And that to me implies qualities of leadership and integrity whether in the fields of social conscience or the encouragement of innovation,' wrote Sir Richard Powell, Director-General of the Institute of Directors, in *The Times* on 29 March 1973. He was defending the findings of a recent survey which established that British directors rated leadership, integrity and knowledge of the business as ranking higher in the list of a board's requirements for its members than ability to innovate, an inquiring mind, social conscience and knowledge of other businesses.

But what is integrity? A certain mystery surrounds the word. Few men or women can define it; most have recognised the reality in another person at one time or another. Some search for its elusive essence. Mountain explorer Eric Shipton in his autobiography *That Untravelled World* (1969) mentioned such a person:

> Kurt Hahn once told me that for ten years he had sought a definition of 'integrity', and had at last found one that satisfied him: 'The triumph over self-swindle.' I asked him if, in his view, I could rob a bank and still retain my integrity; to which he replied, 'Yes, but I wouldn't advise it.' I doubt if the definition would receive general acceptance, but I found it pleasing; for the quality I like most in people is the habit of straight-thinking, of avoiding protective affectation. In the words of one of C. P. Snow's characters, 'Give me the man who knows something of himself and is appalled.' To my mind this is the essence of humility; with it, most faults are tolerable, without it, the noblest virtues become tarnished.

Kurt Hahn's definition could be interpreted as a modern version of the advice of Polonius in *Hamlet*:

> This above all,—To thine own self be true;
> And it must follow, as the night to day,
> Thou canst not then be false to any man.

But supposing my 'self' loves money enough to rob a bank or beat up an old lady in order to get it. Should I still be true to it? Here we touch upon a nerve of our contemporary confusion, i.e. How do I know for sure what is my true self? The principle 'Love self and do as you please' is fine if we can first reach a definition of the self.

The influence of social psychology and sociology has created a sense of ambiguity about the self, and thereby has severely reduced the currency of the word integrity among the young. In particular, sociology's heavy use of the theatrical metaphor of *role* has served to challenge the traditional idea of integrity, as affirmed and believed in by the older generation.

> Role theory, [wrote Professor Peter Berger, a sociologist,] when pursued to its logical conclusions, does far more than provide us with a convenient shorthand for the description of various social activities. It gives us a sociological anthropology, that is, a view of man based on his existence in society. This view tells us that man plays dramatic parts in the grand play of society, and that, speaking sociologically, he *is* the masks that he must wear to do so. The human person also appears now in a dramatic context, true to its theatrical etymology (*persona*, the technical term given to the actors' masks in classical theatre). The person is perceived as a repertoire of roles, each one properly equipped with a certain identity. The range of an individual person can be measured by the number of roles he is capable of playing. The person's biography now appears to us as an uninterrupted sequence of stage performances, played to different audiences, sometimes involving drastic changes of costume, always demanding that the actor *be* what he is playing.
> Such a sociological view of personality is far more radical in its challenge to the way that we commonly think of ourselves than most psychological theories. It challenges radically one of the fondest presuppositions about the self—its continuity. Looked at sociologic-

172

ally, the self is no longer a solid, given entity that moves from one situation to another. It is rather a process, continuously created and re-created in each social situation that one enters, held together by the slender thread of memory. How slender this thread is, we have seen in our discussion of the reinterpretation of the past. Nor is it possible within this framework of understanding to take refuge in the unconscious as containing the 'real' contents of the self, because the presumed unconscious self is just as subject to social production as is the so-called conscious one, as we have seen. In other words, man is not *also* a social being, but he is social in every aspect of his being that is open to empirical investigation. Still speaking sociologically, then, if one wants to ask who an individual 'really' is in this kaleidoscope of roles and identities, one can answer only by enumerating the situations in which he is one thing and those in which he is another.

Thus sociology stops short on the threshold of morality. It cannot answer the question, What is my real self? All it can do is to describe a chameleon-like entity, endlessly adapting itself to situations according to the role it chooses (or is chosen) to play in them. Thus integrity means fidelity to the role or part, whatever that entails in moral terms. But it could be asserted against this modern orthodoxy that what is 'real' or 'unreal' stands close to what is 'good' or 'evil'. So that my real self may be my good self, in the moral sense. And my false self or selves springs to life when I act deliberately in a less than good way. In other words, the struggle for morality is not so much to be good as to be real. And the battle against immorality is in fact the expression of a self-love seeking to avoid a shrinking or even a loss of the true self. Thus the loss of integrity cannot be compared to losing a wallet: it can be equated with a sudden contraction of one's real self.

THE MEANINGS OF INTEGRITY

The primary meaning of integrity comes from its Latin ancestor *integer*, whole. By the middle of the sixteenth century integrity had also acquired its moral sense: 'soundness of moral principle; the character of uncorrupted virtue; uprightness, honesty, sincerity.' Webster's Dictionary expanded this sense to embrace an 'adherence to a code of moral, artistic, or other values'.

Serving the truth, in the fuller sense as a value close to goodness and other than self, is central to the concept of integrity. It means accepting what is true, right or good from whatever quarter it comes. Writing in the obituary columns of *The Times* in 1973 a senior British civil servant could add this footnote on his erstwhile boss:

> Best of all was a remark of his to me which I have always treasured and tried to remember when I myself became a senior. I had mentioned, over tea, that I had just written a long minute to him, and said that I was not at all sure that what I had said was right. 'My dear . . .,' he replied, 'there is no such thing as right and wrong in our work. There is only your opinion and my opinion, and it so happens that, as I am the senior, mine will prevail.' What better *envoi* could any young man have on the threshold of a civil service career?

Fortunately another contributor to *The Times* on that same day gave a possible answer to the last question. Recollecting a conversation with Harry S. Truman when the latter came to Oxford University to receive an honorary degree, a professor recalled that the President told him he had another quotation on his desk, besides the well-known 'The buck stops here.' This was a sentence from Mark Twain: 'Always tell the truth; it will please some people and astonish the rest.'

HOW TO EVADE THE MORAL ISSUE

Like physical health, integrity is often taken for granted until it becomes evident that we are in danger of losing it. What sorts out the human sheep from the inhuman goats is the cost the former are willing to pay for sticking to their moral principles. If the relation between morality and personal wholeness is clearly perceived, then the man or woman undergoing temptation (alias a testing situation) will have to weigh the tangible advantages proffered by the voice of the tempter against the longer-term loss of personal integrity.

Naturally if the temptation is a strong one, if we are straining for it like a starving man in reach of food, then our cunning minds may often deploy various arguments to alter the framework of the experience. Like children, we can swiftly think up some changes in the rules to accommodate our surrender to the test within the boundaries of morality. Herein lies the chief disadvantage of too much emphasis in morality on the uniqueness of each situation: it adds to temptation by providing a ready-made method of justifying a departure from habitual morality. Of course we give ourselves away by being so reluctant to grant others a similar indulgence. Thus, treating ourselves as a 'special case' because of certain features in a situation is one method of trying to preserve our integrity on the grounds that we have maintained our 'morality' intact. But alas for us morality is not primarily about language. What is really done or left undone, even in secret, adds or subtracts from the stature of the real self.

Thus, by rationalisation, we can preserve a nominal integrity. Possibly we have accepted some other person's 'interpretation' of what is moral in such situations in good faith. Or else we may have genuinely deceived ourselves by allowing our 're-interpretation' of morality to happen at a semi-conscious level of the depth mind. However, integrity is not brittle, and it can heal gaping wounds into the scars of experience, provided that the central will to goodness is not broken or wasted slowly away. Evil consumes the muscles of man before it eats out his heart, so there is always time for succour.

Sincerity, or believing in the truth or worth of what is said or done, is therefore a partial preserver of integrity, even though the words or deeds may subsequently be identified as inaccurate or harmful. Honesty may come into play to help a person to know if he is being sincere, or only manipulating the meaning of those values, principles or rules which—in less trying circumstances—he was pleased to serve and perhaps proclaim. Again, the test is what

175

price a person is prepared to pay rather than deny the moral values he has previously accepted and which have informed his character.

Another dubious stratagem is to under-estimate deliberately the consequences of ignoring the warning signs. Based on our knowledge that integrity is resilient, we may decide to chance it 'just this once'. But we never know where a frontier runs in the mountains, or if we shall make our way safely home from a foray into that dark territory which we have long since forbidden ourselves from exploring. The wise person takes no chances, being cautious in Dr Samuel Johnson's definition of the word: 'Provident care, wariness against evil.' The unwary may find themselves in the soft mire of a gradual character disintegration, as the sad picture of drug addicts so painfully poster.

A third possible strategy for seeking to maintain a level of personal integrity without paying the true costs is the semi-conscious compartmentalising of morality and life. So that we allow ourselves to recognise certain areas as emancipated from our personal morality. These may be literally areas, such as foreign countries: 'When in Rome, do as the Romans do.' Or they may be spheres of living, such as business or social life. By closing the bulkhead doors on one part of our life we hope to keep the whole ship afloat. By dividing ourselves, like double-yoked eggs, we do preserve an element of unity. But that total wholeness of personal integrity is left behind. Thus several selves may form on the variant moralities, like ice growing around trailing fishing lines in frozen seas.

THE PRICE OF INTEGRITY

The price of his or her own integrity is fixed by each individual person. Whether or not that price will ever have to be paid is largely outside the individual's control. There were, of course, some hundreds of Germans in Nazi Germany who preferred to lose their physical lives rather than surrender their integrity. They did not alter the rules to fit their case, nor did they entertain any illusions about their fate, nor did they hastily erect fences to shut out the trying sights and sounds. In death they joined a large company in history of those who came to the point where compromise must end or else they would cease to be themselves. Such people have the moral strength to prefer physical execution to the ending of their integrity, for they cannot imagine a human life without it. They exposed in their deaths the meaning of our lives.

Industry and commerce, along with all other forms of employment, do throw up moral issues which test personal integrity. But the cost of maintaining it is usually no more than loss of employment. Quite what that entails will vary according to individual circumstances, from a temporary career set-back to financial ruin. Just as only few deaths are endured solely for the sake of integrity so there are not many resignations submitted on that count alone. Yet the willingness to resign, or to be sacked, is undeniably the price of personal integrity in business.

Once or twice in a career, the honest director or manager may have to face the agonising dilemma between electing to stay and seek to influence the course of events on the one hand, or resigning on grounds of conscience or moral principle. We may naturally dislike the latter option, not only for its obvious consequences in loss of salary, status, and the social company of valued colleagues, but also because it may seem to imply a moral superiority, a 'holier-than-thou' attitude. Charges along these lines managers find especially hard to bear.

Integrity is not free in the sense that there is no price to be paid for it. The possession of it invites trials of its strength, comprehensiveness and consistency. It must be 'fully stretched' by events and people. The cost may be one's job. Or the costs might be measured in love, pleasure, gain, friends, popularity, prospects or money. There is no such thing as cheap goodness.

THE APPEAL TO LOYALTY

A major pressure, both inside the conscience of a middle or junior manager and externally upon him, may be his sense of loyalty to the company. 'Loyal' comes by way of an Old French word from the

Latin *legalis:* legal. Primarily it means to be faithful in allegiance to one's lawful government. Secondly, however, it embraces being true or faithful to a private person to whom fidelity is held to be due. Thus loyalty has chiefly a meaning of response to the obligations of the constituted government, as established under law, and a semi-metaphorical use for faithful devotion to a person, family, group or organisation. The bridge between these two usages was the person of the medieval sovereign, who was held to embody the law.

A deep conflict of loyalties is difficult to resolve or bear. In business it most commonly afflicts managers whose loyalty to their boss or the company (a person under the law) is set at variance with their sense of loyalty to the moral law, whether or not it is reflected by clauses on the Statute Book. If it is so codified the troubled manager may appeal to it, but the knowledge that the law of the land supports him may not assuage the agonies of disrupted relationships. There may be a way of acting which does least damage to the network of loyalties which has developed over the years. But in the last resort the man of integrity will make it plain that his loyalties to superiors, groups, and organisations—even society and the state—are not his ultimate ones. It seems to be in us that we can love ideals or values. If they define the nature of reality, of course, then our loyalty to this order actually complements or fulfils all other loyalties, despite the *apparent* conflict between them. To his lady love, who protested at his going to fight in the English Civil War, the Cavalier poet Richard Lovelace penned these immortal lines:

> I could not love thee, Dear, so much,
> Loved I not Honour more.

Loyalty to people or institutions is a fine quality, which arouses our admiration and respect. But it is a part and not the whole of morality. In order to understand and exercise it aright, we have to set our loyalty to persons and organisations within the context of a much larger framework of values. It is adherence to this framework which both expresses and creates integrity.

THE ADVANTAGES OF INTEGRITY

Having described the difficulties which may roughen 'the steep and thorny way' of integrity, it is only fair to point out some of the beneficial effects of integrity in personal and public life. For we persuade ourselves to be moral more by painting the attractions of goodness than by stressing the dire consequences of immoral behaviour.

1. *Freedom*

Several managers who took part in the Baumhart survey on business ethics observed that good practice freed you from time-consuming worry, fears and guilt. Since time is a precious resource in any personal or corporate working life this particular effect is not to be despised. Saving time may seem a strange reason for being moral, but anyone on the road to—or from—goodness knows how many days and hours can be wasted in extricating oneself and others from a perplexing moral muddle. Of course some people enjoy such dramas and their reflective aftermaths, but they do not on the whole make good business managers.

The old optical illusion of morality—when the gate marked freedom leads into a prison while the door of self-limitation opens upon wide plains of experience—still deceives us, though we have tried them a hundred times. The truth can be tested in industry and commerce by measuring the long-term freedom to operate enjoyed by a company. Bad practice leads to loss of freedom as reputation spreads; good business dealing ever widens the potential market. Also individual managers can measure the time involved in the alternative strategies. Morality can be almost defined as that which you can do without thinking about it afterwards. Therefore its 'service is perfect freedom'. Consistency conserves decision-making time.

2. *Trust*

Mutual trust is the basis of positive human relationships, be they personal or professional ones.

Personal Integrity

It is a fact that integrity tends to create trust, while conduct void of it results in a growing mistrust. The roots of this fact doubtless lie in the mysterious sub-soil of our common human nature, and speculation about them need not detain us here. But it is a universal observation that good people are trustworthy, and are often trusted. Of course there are many other factors in a situation, industrial or otherwise, besides the probity of the parties concerned. But people are extraordinarily sensitive to personal and professional integrity, and when they perceive its presence they acknowledge it with trust.

The cumulative effects of a disregard for integrity upon the level of trust in an organisation received notice in an article in *International Business* entitled 'Do your employees believe in you?' The British Institute of Management published this summary of its findings:

> One senior manager in a large organisation looked forward to joining his new company, finding its talk of regular appraisals, merit increases, promotion from within, etc., stirring stuff. He soon found himself questioning why these were so delayed and why rises for his own staff, however slight, were put aside so inevitably. He was told that it was company policy to offer high wages, frequent rises and so on, and yet to systematically delay or deny them at the operative time. It was, in short, company policy to ignore company policy. It saved money.
>
> When the confidence of employees in their management wanes, respect and esteem for them may never be regained. For it is possible to possess all the elements of effective management save one—credibility—and the lack of this one will doom an enterprise to failure. Some of the more obvious factors in opening up a credibility gap are: a disparity between words and deeds; the systematic use of words to conceal motives; uncertainty among men in authority, and lack of contact between a leader and his employees.
>
> The four remedies are therefore quite clear. A manager should keep every commitment, act predictably, be consistent with his own philosophy in doing as he says he will and lastly encourage the airing of dissent so that solutions are found.

Besides the importance of trust in industrial relations there is an increasing recognition that it matters in any working group. In an article entitled 'Trust and Managerial Problem Solving', which appeared in *Administrative Science Quarterly* during 1972, Dale E. Zand of the New York University Business School reported some research where groups of business executives were given identical factual information about a difficult manufacturing-marketing policy problem: half the groups were briefed to expect trusting behaviour and the other half to expect untrusting behaviour. 'There were highly significant differences in effectiveness between the high-trust groups and the low-trust groups in the clarification of goals, the reality of information exchanged, the scope of search for solutions, and the commitment of managers to implement solutions. The findings indicate that shared trust or lack of trust apparently are a significant determinant of managerial problem-solving effectiveness.'

Clearly the integrity of the leader (or senior management) will reduce occasions for mistrust. For example, members will not be punished for speaking the truth, for integrity implies a prior commitment to the truth wherever it is to be found. Integrity helps to create the optimum climate for decision-making, problem-solving or creative thinking.

3. *Vision*

The third effect of integrity is less obviously related to it than either freedom or trust. What is vision? Within the context of working organisations it has two main meanings. First, with reference to the future, it is an act of the imagination in which something is seen in a distinct and vivid way. A far-sighted person can see events or trends and their consequences some considerable distance into the future, but a man of vision will be the more creative because his imaginative picture may help to form that uncreated future. Therefore vision is not the antithesis of reality. Today's vision is tomorrow's reality. Of course in order to realise that vision managers have to persuade others that it is eminently worthy of a place in the mosaic of tomorrow's world. Without this touchstone of reality a person of vision relapses into being merely a visionary.

Secondly, vision is the special sense by which we perceive the qualities of an object, such as colour, luminosity, shape and size, that together constitute its appearance and nature. For the manager the object in question will be his organisation. His vision of it may be compounded of an insight into its distinctive characteristics, coupled with a lively sense of it as a living body which is more than a sum of its constituent parts. In other words, he will have an awareness of its integrity as well as its several divisions, functions or departments.

CAN INTEGRITY BE LEARNT ?

Integrity obviously cannot be taught like mathematics, although it is possible to stir up the natural awareness of its importance by imaginative training methods. A film such as Robert Bolt's *A Man for All Seasons*, a remarkably accurate study of the life of Sir Thomas More, achieved that result while becoming also a box-office success. An older Royal Canadian Air Force film called *Integrity* portrayed a young navigator who had cheated in examinations and with an engaging smile then lied his way out of being blamed for a car accident. What does he do when he finds himself on a trans-arctic flight having forgotten to bring some vital aeronautical tables ? At first he seeks to bluff, but his dilemma grows as it becomes clearer that the aircraft is flying off course into danger . . . Such open-ended films allow students ample room to discuss and discover the wider range of integrity, once they have encountered the elementary demands of honesty and willingness to admit mistakes.

Morality can be partly learnt from other people and from digesting our experience of the persistence of moral considerations in human life. But we have not troubled enough to understand how people develop a moral sensibility, and in particular the role which the unconscious or depth mind plays in the process. The lives of saints, for example, often exhibit three phases. First comes a period of moral endeavour, where the person is earnestly trying to live up to the demands of morality. This time, which may last many years, is succeeded by a confused period of heart-searching and the reluctant admission of failure, accompanied by emotions of anxiety and despair. In this darkness there stands out a star of hope or the slow dawn of a new day. What once seemed an external and impossible moral law, bent on compressing and killing the self, now comes as the heart's desire, the free expression of a humbled and good spirit.

CONCLUSION

There is a sense in which integrity can be envisaged as a defensive or negative device, like a suit of expensive Milanese armour: proof against swords and arrows, superbly articulated yet always possessing weak joints or links. An owner of such richly-ornamented and valuable clothing may well feel justly proud of it, and sensitive to any aspersions about its comprehensiveness or beauty. He may even be tempted to boast about it in a morally self-righteous way. But, married to humility and securely hidden like a hair-shirt, integrity does have the same defensive function for the spirit and mind as armour has for the body.

Yet integrity is the hallmark of a person who is actively pursuing good ends which he values more than himself. Therefore it is a vital attribute for leaders in a social capitalist society already on the move towards a morally and socially better world. In a 1970 *Observer* interview between Kenneth Harris and Sir Ernest Woodroofe, chairman of Unilever, this need for a positive and potentially costing response to the *whole* value structure of social capitalism received a clear and succinct expression:

Harris: What single quality makes an industrial leader?
Woodroofe: No single quality, but an indispensable one is integrity. No doubt about it. Assuming certain qualities like efficiency, imagination, shrewdness, doggedness and so on, the all-essential one is integrity.
Harris: What do you mean by integrity in this context?

Personal Integrity

Woodroofe: Most decisions in business are based on uncertainties because you don't have all the information you would theoretically like to have, but having what you have, you must use your judgement and decide. But, and this is what I mean by the overriding importance of integrity, the decision must be made within the framework of the responsibilities the businessman carries. He has responsibilities to the shareholders, the employees, the consumer, even the government of the day. He has to balance these responsibilities thoroughly, justly and without bias. You could, for instance, make a decision which was to the benefit of your shareholders but to the detriment of the community as a whole. *Not* doing that, and knowing why you are not going to do it, and what not doing it is going to cost you, is what I mean by integrity.

Conclusion

This book has fallen into two parts. The first five chapters traced
the rise of the particular complexion of values which have led us to
the threshold of what I will call social capitalism. My method
has been to take each of the major values separately, and show how
it comes to us with a pedigree of moral (or immoral) associations.
Then I attempted to discern the way in which these cardinal values
related to each other, using a simple visual model of the over-
lapping circles in Chapter 5.

The first main value—or cluster of values—concerns the
equivalent exchange of goods and services, money and profit-
making. Money and financial profit were the comparative late-
comers in this trinity, both fraught with moral consequence. The
other values, present implicitly from the start but unfolding more
slowly than money, are respectively society, the individual and
nature. Each of these, like money itself, has acquired and lost
religious overtones in the course of their long histories. Business
comes to us out of the mists of early times already set firmly
within the context of human world-views and moral ideas. The
frameworks have changed, but not the basic belief that business
belongs within a wider order which is inherently moral. Working
on a small canvas of five chapters, and faced with the vast and
intricate panorama of history, I could obviously do no more than
sketch rapidly an outline, dash in some colours and add some
details, trusting the reader will both forgive the degree of carica-
ture and complete or modify the picture from the stores of his own
knowledge and imagination.

But the view of the historian or philosopher is that of the

observer on the outside looking in, or contemplating at a distance the many facets of a complex and living system. In fact we are all participants in social capitalism. We are born into it and educated in the schools and colleges made possible by its wealth. As consumers, employees, citizens, and shareholders (if only by way of government or pension funds) we are inextricably involved in the web or fabric of our socio-economic system. The stance of an entirely disinterested observer is not open to us. Those who pose as such, often in the name of science, are merely unmindful of the reality of their lives. Of course we need to make the effort towards an objective understanding which is true science, but in this sphere the observer constantly has to remind himself that he himself is part of the evidence, that he is totally committed or implicated in the present and uncreated future of social capitalism. As Marcuse said: 'If you are not part of the solution, you are part of the problem.'

This feeling will perhaps be stronger in those who are directly involved in industry or commerce, such as managers. For they are the frontiersmen of social capitalism. Its future will be actualised one way or the other not by such books as this one, but by the cumulative drift of countless decisions, falling like flakes of snow on the silent mountain tops. In the second half of the book, therefore, the focus of attention shifted to the proverbial 'man in the hot seat': the manager, politician or trade union leader who is faced with the making of those daily but significant decisions across the broad and moving frontier which we call the present.

Perhaps the hardest moral decisions are not those which call for a choice between good and evil, despite the endless fascinations of the latter. Rather we are most tested when we have to choose between two different values, each of which we recognise as good in its own way. From the history of social capitalism and its plural value structure, it is clear that there are and will be constantly recurring situations where a leader finds himself faced with such dilemmas. How can he be helped?

First, we have to understand how any human mind works when

faced with issues of this nature. In Chapter 6 these reactions were arranged in some order, but it is not possible or even desirable to suggest a tidy 'drill' for all situations. Among the more useful tools in the moral problem-solver's bag is the tradition of his trade in resolving similar ethical questions as framed in the form of a code or set of rules. The quest for such a code in the sphere of business management formed the subject of Chapter 7.

Yet codes have to be learnt and their uses within the much larger framework of moral judgement understood. Chapter 8 discussed the place of the broad value structure of social capitalism and its consequent moral obligations within the context of management education and training. To place too much faith on either formal codes or the efficacy of education, however, is to ignore those research findings which identify the key position of the top leadership in setting and maintaining the moral character of an enterprise. In Chapter 9 I have weighed some of the current proposals for influencing the company board of directors in the light of their undisputed role as policy decision-makers in social and moral matters as well as in the technical conduct of the business.

Yet the last word in any discussion of moral action must return to the individual. Books, codes, superiors or colleagues may provide guides or models, but the ultimate responsibility still rests with the individual. He is answerable for his own decisions, if only to himself. Consequently Chapter 10 considered anew the relevance of personal integrity in business.

More than once I have found myself mentioning the need to find new motives for old. Somehow we have to unleash more of the vast human potential energy for good. It is by re-thinking our ideas of wealth, profit and gain that our motivation may possibly receive its new computer programme. Profit comes from the Latin word *profectus*, advance. We need now to reclaim boldly this larger sense and define what we mean by *advance* or progress. It may include financial profits and the growth in national wealth and corporate size, but these limited ideals will hardly suffice the truly proficient manager of tomorrow. We should expect to see some creative experiments toward 'value added' motives, based upon the historic assumption that work should be first and foremost the method whereby we satisfy our creature needs (through money as means of exchange), fulfil our reciprocal nature as givers and receivers, and express in our various contributions what we already are as unique 'children of the universe'.

The relation of management and morality is far from new. The presence of ethical ideas in the conduct of business affairs is older than the Bible. Still further back we may assume that the primitive ethic, based on the reciprocity of human nature, provided some simple homespun moral rules for our ancestors in their early societies. Coming back to our own century, we have seen repeated efforts to advance the philosophy of social responsibility through the introduction of codes of business ethics. The essential values and much of the subject-matter of these statements and codes are certainly not new, except in the sense that as gold never rusts so goodness never grows old.

The novelty of today's emerging management ethic lies less in its parts than in its depths and range. It is the whole pattern of ideas, laws, and informal codes fusing into a common approach as the profession of management matures that is new. The interaction of practice and ideas, powered by new sources of motive energy, has directed our minds towards the next remaining great challenges in our society, which are the moral ones.

To be good a person must be free to be bad. For morality embraces motive and choice, as well as action and its consequences. An externally imposed morality ceases to be moral if it invades this area of legitimate freedom. Therefore we should shun the vision of an ethical bureaucracy; codes administered by qualified inquisitors will issue only in corporate hypocrisy and personal humbug. We should rather look upon social capitalism as a laboratory for human goodness, where we can experiment and learn from each other.

If we can move towards a general common consciousness of the ends really sought in our society, then paradoxically we can do with fewer rules and less regulations. A guiding set of stars is worth a thousand dated maps. But the prudent voyager, who can find his bearings by lining up the stars in that galaxy, will also equip himself with the navigation rules which we call business ethics. The latter should concentrate on the practices which are acceptable to business and society at large.

The leaders of tomorrow will combine a high degree of technical competence and knowledge with the ability to articulate and make concrete the values which together disclose our emerging common social purpose. They should communicate with us not only about the advantages they would guide us towards, but also about the demands of the upward path. Such leaders will therefore need both vision and moral courage. Society expects them to be tough, for there is a formidable task to be accomplished, but ruthless with no one except themselves. For the movement towards goodness contains challenge, effort and personal cost which they must not hide from us all. The message of social capitalism is that we are launched upon that journey without hope of going back. Good leaders increase our chances of making a success of this planet against all the odds.

Yet leadership does not mean going it alone, or impatiently deserting the present for the future. Leaders may place themselves in front of the main body of business and society, but not so far in advance that they lose touch. They belong with the people, and never more so than in the testing times that lie ahead. For, as John Collier wrote some forty years ago: 'Not geniuses, but average men require profound stimulation, incentive towards creative effort and the nurture of great hopes.'